"Part detective story, part therapeutic memoir, *The Outsider* combines the dispassionate tone of a good reporter with the clear-eyed compassion for the father he lost."   —*Toronto Globe and Mail*

"*The Outsider* is a truly wonderful book—a haunting, poignant story of a son's life with, and without, his father. In a mature and fascinating rendering, Lachenmeyer describes the gradual, bewildering, and relentless transformation of his father from a brilliant sociology professor to a frightening victim of paranoid schizophrenia and alcoholism. Lachenmeyer presents a rare and moving portrait of one of life's major struggles—the devastation created by severe mental illness."   —John Olden, M.D., Director,
New York State Psychiatric Institute

"A powerful memoir... a moving account of a son who finds the father he never knew; a brave man, fighting as best he could, against an incurable mental illness."
—Laurence Chollet, *Bergen County Record*

"Poignant and compelling..."   —*Daily Press*

"A remarkable memoir...This extraordinary book [is] one of the best about schizophrenia to have come out in recent years."
—*NAMI Advocate*

"[Written] with compassion and candor... a heartrending portrait."
—*Publishers Weekly*

"*The Outsider* is not just an exploration of mental illness. It's a story about guilt and regret, culminating in a plea for people to rethink how they respond to the transients they pass on the street."
—*New Hampshire Sunday News*

"In *The Outsider*, [Lachenmeyer] serves up a plate of reality with the timing and sense of a novel. The end result is an informative and very enjoyable read which can't fail to touch even the remotest heart."   —*New Reviews Newletter*

"How does a man with a Ph.D. in sociology end up as a homeless vagrant with paranoid schizophrenia? His son wondered too, and this is his poignant and painful story. It is a well-written and brave account that reminds us of the faces behind the masks of the homeless. Highly recommended."

"Unlike depression, a topic only now coming out of the closet, people with schizophrenia continue to be social outcasts—blamed, stigmatized, and very much alone. With his honest, unsentimentalized account, Nathaniel Lachenmeyer has gone an extraordinary way toward breaking the silence and throwing light on their world through a child's unconditionally loving eyes."

"In *The Outsider*...Lachenmeyer pieces together an honest and often painful story exposing our own deep fears of mental illness. This ability to show us the human being behind the label of schizophrenia is what makes this book so compelling."

"*The Outsider* chronicles the effects of this cruel and savage disorder with dispassion, sensitivity, and intelligence. This compelling tragedy cannot be equaled by any account of psychiatric illness that I have encountered to date."

"At moments funny, oftentimes sad, but always unflinchingly honest, Lachenmeyer's poignant memoir ultimately offers us a portrait of the mentally ill and homeless that we rarely, if ever, see."

"Lachenmeyer followed his father's path as it descended into the underworld of flop houses, park benches, and long, lonely winter days in New England, where the elder Lachenmeyer drifted after leaving Pelham. It is a portrait of madness as seen through the eyes of a son."

"Nathaniel Lachenmeyer's unstinting account of his passionate search for his father's story explains much about schizophrenia, but more about how the mysterious confluence of genetics and life experience makes us who we are."

The Outsider

The Outsider

A Journey

into My

Father's

Struggle

with

Madness

Nathaniel Lachenmeyer

Broadway Books

New York

A hardcover edition of this book was published in 2000 by Broadway Books.

THE OUTSIDER. Copyright © 2000 by Nathaniel Lachenmeyer. All rights reserved. Printed in the United States of America. No part of this book may be reproduced or transmitted in any form or by any means, electronic or mechanical, including photocopying, recording, or by any information storage and retrieval system, without written permission from the publisher. For information, address Broadway Books, a division of Random House, Inc., 1540 Broadway, New York, NY 10036.

Broadway Books titles may be purchased for business or promotional use or for special sales. For information, please write to: Special Markets Department, Random House, Inc., 1540 Broadway, New York, NY 10036.

BROADWAY BOOKS and its logo, a letter B bisected on the diagonal, are trademarks of Broadway Books, a division of Random House, Inc.

Visit our website at www.broadwaybooks.com

First Broadway Books trade paperback edition published 2001.

Designed by Pei Loi Koay

The photo of New Hampshire State Hospital on page 6 of the insert appears by permission of the New Hampshire Historical Society (#F1234).

The Library of Congress has cataloged the hardcover edition as follows:
Lachenmeyer, Nathaniel, 1969–
The Outsider: a journey into my father's struggle with madness/by
Nathaniel Lachenmeyer.—1st ed.
p.   cm.
1. Lachenmeyer, Charles William, 1943–1995—Mental health.
2. Schizophrenia—Patients—United States—Biography.
3. Mental illness—Patients—United States—Biography.   I. Title.

RC514.L23 2000
616.89′82′0092—dc21
[B]
99-051796

ISBN 0-7679-0191-6

10 9 8 7 6 5 4

For Charles William Lachenmeyer

1943–1995

*For the multitude of men and women
with schizophrenia living on the streets
of New York City, who remind me
every day that this book is about the
present as much as it is about the past.*

None of us can help the things life has

done to us. They're done before you

realize it, and once they're done they

make you do other things until at last

everything comes between you and

what you'd like to be, and you've lost

your true self forever.

—Eugene O'Neill,
  Long Day's Journey into Night

Contents

Acknowledgments

I would like to thank the following people, whose assistance made this book possible.

The people who agreed to tell me what they remembered about my father—

The people who knew him in New York. Clifford Eriksen, Paul Feinstein, Dr. Theodore Kemper, James McKenzie, Dr. John Oldham, Tom Salvator, George Sherman, Herbert Teitelbaum.

The people who knew him in Virginia. Dr. Brian Chabot, Dudley Jensen, Dr. Wayne Kernodle, Dr. Edwin Rhyne, Waldemar Riley, Richard Wolfson, Shomer Zwelling.

The people who knew him in North Carolina. Dr. Richard Cramer, Dr. Satoshi Ito, Dr. Jim Wiggins.

The people who knew him in New Hampshire. Debbie Becker, Sean Chandler, George Comtois, Susan Deane, Diane DiStaso, Dr. Robert Drake, John Englund, Jolyon Johnson, Helena Laware, Kratz

Leatherman, Barbara Maloney, Anne Nute, John O'Malley, Gail Page, Eleanor Rager, Dr. Edward Rowen, Janet Stiles, Ralph Twombly, Dr. Robert Vidaver.

The people who knew him in Vermont. Corporal Robert Booher, Dr. John Burchard, Mike Cohen, Barbara Collins, Officer Frederick Colvin, Robert Conlon, Kimball Daigneault, Steven Danaher, Jeffrey Degree, Detective Daniel Doherty, Daniel Forsey, Louis Hines, Ruth Hunt, Amy King, John Lapp, Helen Leary, David Lines, John Lines, Henry Mack, John Markey, Mark Martin, James Morgan, Dr. Richard Munson, H. P. Palmer, Jason Palmer, Willis Racht, Allison Sarno, Jerry Schwarz, Gary Sisco, Judge Marilyn Skoaglund, Dr. Sandra Steingard, Officer Kathleen Stubbing, Laura Thompson, Dr. William Woodruff.

The people who helped sustain me during the difficult times—

My mother, whose support, encouragement, honesty, and strength are responsible for much of what is good in this book and much of what is good in me. My wife, Christina, whose love, kindness, and generosity have restored my interest in the future. Juliana Bates, whose friendship saved me from seeing my father's image in death. Georgie, Inside-Outside, Pythias, Damian, Desirée, Poa, Mr. Jones, and Stanley—who have taught me that good friends often walk on four legs.

Author's Note

This book is about my father. This book is also about schizophrenia. Approximately 1 percent of the population worldwide suffers from schizophrenia—an estimated 2.5 million people in the U.S. alone. More than one hundred thousand new cases are reported here each year. The age of onset, although variable, is generally late adolescence or early adulthood. The diagnosis of schizophrenia involves the recognition of a constellation of signs and symptoms associated with impaired occupational and social functioning. Contrary to popular belief, schizophrenia has nothing to do with multiple personality disorder. Symptoms include: delusions, hallucinations, disorganized speech, grossly disorganized or catatonic behavior, and flattening of affect. Approximately one-third of people with schizophrenia, my father included, suffer from the paranoid subtype, which is distinguished by prominent delusions and/or auditory hallucinations, usually organized around a common theme, without prominent disturbances in cognitive functioning or affect.

Schizophrenia is one of the most chronic and debilitating of all mental illnesses, accounting for more than three thousand deaths per year in the US, 93 percent from suicide. The overall lifetime suicide rate for people with schizophrenia is more than 10 percent; approximately half of people diagnosed with schizophrenia will make a suicide attempt at some point during their lives. Mortality in persons with schizophrenia is two to four times higher than in the general population. Measured in economic terms, the disorder costs the US 32.5 billion dollars annually in direct treatment and support costs, loss of productivity, and caregiver and related services. More than any other human affliction, schizophrenia defines the character of the American city, accounting—with bipolar disorder—for approximately one-third of the homeless population in the US.

As a result of their disorder, people with schizophrenia typically function at a much lower level than they had prior to the onset of symptoms. Many individuals are unable to hold a job for sustained periods of time and are employed at lower levels than their parents—a phenomenon known as "downward drift." The majority of individuals with schizophrenia do not marry, and most have relatively limited social contacts. Many have limited or no insight into the fact that they are ill. Most studies suggest that the course the disorder takes is variable from case to case, with some individuals displaying exacerbations and remissions, and others remaining chronically ill. Complete remission is rare.

There are many competing theories about the causes of schizophrenia. There is a general consensus, however, that schizophrenia is a neurobiological disorder; that is, that its causes are primarily biological rather than social in nature. The main methods of treatment for schizophrenia are antipsychotic medications, which act on the neurotransmitters in the brain, complemented with occupational and social skills training and supportive psychotherapy. Although antipsychotic medications have become much more effective in treating some of the symptoms of schizophrenia over the past three decades—in particular, delusions and hallucinations—their efficacy is not uniform for all people suffering from schizophrenia, and they can be attended by severe side effects. Most people with schizophrenia continue to suffer some symptoms throughout their lives irrespective of the method of treatment. There is no cure for schizophrenia.

The Outsider

Part One

We all leave behind memories as our

primary legacy.

—Charles Lachenmeyer,
  Thought Control and Technological
  Slavery in America (?), Issue 1

Chapter 1

The
Transient

I still remember the shock I felt the first time I saw the transient. It was December 1, 1978, the day before my ninth birthday. It was snowing. My father and I were on our annual excursion to a camera store on the West Side of Manhattan that sold Super 8 movies. Each year at my birthday party, after lunch and cake, my father would set up the S-8 movie projector and portable screen in the cramped quarters of his wood-paneled office. With the help of six or seven kids, darkness, and a little imagination, my father's office acquired the magic of an old movie palace. In one afternoon we would see Charlie Chaplin in *The Circus*, Bela Lugosi in *Dracula*, and Boris Karloff and Vincent Price battling in *The Raven*—all conveniently shortened to fit the S-8 format, which allowed us to get in a game of kickball before it got too dark. The last movie my father threaded through the projector was always the new addition to the collection.

My father and I spent an hour at the store poring over the horror movie selection—our favorite category. In the end, we could not decide between *One Million BC* and *Frankenstein*, so we chose *Them* instead, the cult classic about giant radioactive ants. We promised ourselves that the following year we would pick a comedy. After we left the store, we tested the accumulated snow's snowball potential and found it lacking. When my father asked me what I would like to do next, he could not keep from smiling; he knew what I would say. Twenty years later the American Museum of Natural History is still one of my favorite destinations.

Although I grew up only thirty minutes north of Manhattan, in Pelham, a small town on the Westchester-Bronx border, I remember my trips to the city with my father as the big adventures of my childhood. I felt happy and proud walking along the crowded streets, holding my father's hand. We were never out-of-towners visiting the big city; we were conquerors surveying our domain. Climbing the wide steps to the museum entrance, my heart began to race with excitement. We walked by the sixty-three-foot-long canoe filled with replicas of Northwest Coast Indians without so much as a glance, ignored Birds of the World and African Peoples, and did not stop until we arrived at the Carl Akeley Hall of African Mammals, where we spent the afternoon staring back at the glass-eyed stuffed elephants, lions, and antelopes. I could talk about animals all day at that age, and my father seemed to share my affliction.

Later, in the Hall of Ocean Life, walking back and forth under my favorite display—the life-size replica of a female Blue Whale that hung suspended from the ceiling—I told my father one of my greatest secrets: I had decided that I liked animals better than people. I expected him to be shocked and impressed by my declaration. Instead, he smiled, kissed me on the forehead, and said that sometimes he felt the same way.

We ended our visit at the display that scared me too much to qualify as my favorite, but just enough to be captivating: in low lighting that suggested the ocean depths, a sperm whale and a giant squid were engaged in a battle to the death. Pressing myself up against the glass, I told my father that the sperm whale was my favorite whale because it had teeth. My father told me that his favorite was the humpback whale because of its songs. We stared for a few more minutes at the awesome scene, then my father reminded me that we were expected home for dinner.

After taking the subway to Times Square, we decided to walk across 42nd Street to Grand Central Station rather than transfer to the Shuttle. We had not yet given up on the idea of playing in the snow. As we climbed out of the subway, holding hands, feeling good about our day and what we had accomplished, the transient appeared. He was very tall, almost as tall as my father, and very thin, with long unkempt hair, a matted beard, and dirty, ill-fitting clothes. A fine layer of snow had collected on the shoulders of his coat, in his hair, and in his beard. I could smell him from where he stood. I was not scared until he tried to speak to us. His voice terrified me. His breath came out as puffs of smoke. He spoke quickly and sounded angry. My father pulled me away before what he said had a chance to register.

The streetlight stopped us at the corner. I held my breath, tucked in my chin, and looked back slowly over my shoulder. He was standing in exactly the same spot, talking and gesticulating furiously in the falling snow, as if he still saw us standing at the entrance of the subway, listening attentively. I squeezed my father's hand and leaned into him, grateful for his presence. I knew instinctively that I was witnessing something terrible, something that was not supposed to be. There is something unnatural about a man talking out loud to no one at all. It violates a basic principle of human behavior: when you talk, you talk to someone. The light changed. I kept looking back over my shoulder as we crossed the street. Sensing my fear, my father explained in a low voice that once in a while a person can get lost in his thoughts the way he or I might get lost walking in the city.

From that day on, every time I visited Manhattan I saw the transient. His face changed, but his uniform always remained the same: weathered skin, soiled clothes, scraggly hair. Eventually, the alchemy of time transformed my fear into irritation and indifference. The transient slipped quietly out of my consciousness, entering the part of the mind that is reserved for the commonplace. He became a fact of urban living, no more no less, like rush hour or taxis.

On the evening of January 2, 1995, a fifty-one-year-old man died of a heart attack in a decrepit second-floor apartment on Church Street in Burlington, Vermont— a small city three hundred miles north of New York City. The landlord found him the next morning on the floor by the bed and called the police. Police dispatch responded by sending an officer over to investigate. After inspecting the body, the officer turned his attention to the apartment, which was uncharacteristically run-down for downtown Burlington. The more he looked around the more curious he became about the dead man lying on the floor. The water-damaged plaster, the stained, worn-out carpeting, the absence of a kitchenette or hot plate, and the thrift store furniture all suggested extreme poverty. In contrast to this, sitting on top of a small bookshelf by the bed was a neatly arranged stack of paper—copies of the man's résumé. The officer was surprised to learn that the dead man had been a professor—a sociologist—and had written books. Education was supposed to ward off this kind of ending.

The officer walked over to one of the two small windows in the opposite wall and opened it a couple of inches to offset the heat from the radiators. Movement on Church Street caught his eye. Several families with skis in tow were walking slowly up the street, their children zigzagging in front of them excitedly. The children's voices came in with the cold air. In front of the window was a folding card table cluttered with several containers of Chinese take-out, four empty beer cans, a plastic cup overflowing with cigarette butts, and a pile of opened mail. The officer looked through the mail and found a half-dozen rejection letters from colleges to which the man had recently applied for teaching positions. Fanned out on the floor in front of a moldy armchair by the other window were several academic-sounding books checked out from the local library, a tourist guide to Burlington with a photograph of New Year's Eve fireworks on the cover, and the alumni directories of the Poly Preparatory Country Day School in Brooklyn and the College of William and Mary in Virginia.

Half hidden by the William and Mary directory was a large spiral notebook filled with notes written in a tiny uneven scrawl. The officer was still thumbing through the spiral notebook when the medical examiner arrived. "It doesn't make sense," the officer said, half to himself, half to the medical examiner. "The condition of the place and this unlimited vocabulary he has written up in a notebook. An intelligent man like this gets down to this point—how did he get to be in *this* apartment in *Burlington, Vermont?*"

After returning to the police station, the officer did a

background check on the man. His police record consisted of a string of citations for misdemeanor crimes like trespassing, panhandling, and theft of services. Most of the crimes were committed over a four-month period during the winter of 1993. The record revealed that the apartment he was living in at the time of his death was actually a significant improvement over his living conditions the year before: from March 1993 through January 1994 he had been homeless, living on the streets of Burlington.

When the officer pulled the man's file he was shocked by his arrest photograph. The man in the photograph had been a notorious transient on Church Street; his name had been known to every beat cop in the downtown area. He bore little resemblance, however, to the man on the floor of the apartment on Church Street. The man in the photograph had long, scraggly dark hair and a big bushy beard, and was wearing a soiled winter coat. The dead man was clean-shaven, had neatly trimmed hair, and was wearing inexpensive but conservative slacks, an oxford shirt, and dress socks. The officer confirmed that they were the same man by checking the statistics on the back of the arrest photograph. Both the man in the photograph and the man on Church Street were Caucasian, had brown-gray hair and hazel eyes, and were approximately six-feet four-inches tall. The description matched in every respect except one. The man the officer had seen in the apartment weighed about 210 pounds; the weight of the man in the photograph was listed as 140 pounds. Seeing those statistics, the officer realized that the transient had almost starved to death living on the street the year before.

Later that day, the medical examiner called the officer to give him the results of the autopsy: the cause of death was heart disease; the manner of death was natural. All that remained to be done was to locate the next of kin. A card in the man's wallet indicated that at the time of his death he had been a client at the Howard Center for Human Services, a nonprofit social service agency in Burlington. The officer called the staff at the Howard Center and learned that the dead man had been involuntarily committed to Vermont State Hospital in Waterbury on January 26, 1994, following his arrest on a panhandling charge. His diagnosis upon admission was paranoid schizophrenia. He was subsequently stabilized on psychiatric medication and released at the end of November, five weeks before his death.

When the officer heard the words "paranoid schizophrenia," the inconsistencies in the case suddenly seemed less confusing. Over the years he had responded to many complaints against mentally ill transients, usually for misdemeanor crimes like those committed by the man. From time to time a transient would, while protesting his innocence, lay claim to an impressive array of past accomplishments, but the officer had always dismissed this as delusional fantasy. He had never been able until now to corroborate their claims; nor had he ever had any reason to connect their diminished present circumstances to a past—a time before they were, simply, the transient.

The staff at the Howard Center told the officer that a first cousin, Clifford Eriksen, was listed in his psychiatric records from Vermont State Hospital as his family contact. There were also several references in the records to an ex-wife and a son. No contact information was available, however, for his ex-wife or son, and the records indicated that he had been out of touch with them for several years. The officer called Clifford and informed him of his cousin's death, bringing the case to a close. Clifford called my mother. My mother called me.

I was living in Manhattan when my father died—the destination for so many of our old adventures, and the dominion of the transient. The night before his funeral I dreamed about the day in 1978 when I first saw the transient. In the dream I saw myself from a distance— an eight-year-old boy standing alone on a street corner, looking back over his shoulder. The transient was standing at the entrance to the subway, shouting and gesticulating furiously, not to himself, but to me. I could not understand what he was saying and he did not look at all like my father, but somehow I knew that he *was* my father, and that that was what he was trying to tell me. I wanted to tell him that I knew, but I could not move or speak. I just stood there helplessly, watching him. The dream went on and on all night long with him trying to tell me and me standing there mute and the streetlight blinking red and green.

Before falling asleep, I had forced myself to reread in chronological order all of the letters I had received from my father over the years. I wanted to find something appropriate to read at the service I had planned for the following day. I also wanted to examine critically my handling of our relationship over the years, which, following my parents' divorce in 1981, had consisted almost entirely of correspondence. I saw my father only twice after the divorce. He called often, but his behavior was so strange and disturbing that my mother was forced to keep the answering machine on in the house twenty-four hours a day. She tried to censor his letters as well, but she was not always able to get to the mail before me. There were twenty letters in all, the first dated 1982, the last dated 1991, four years before my father's death.

The letters arrived sporadically, on average one every few months, and were usually accompanied by bizarre and frightening enclosures: self-published delusional pamphlets that attempted to prove the existence of a widespread conspiracy to steal his independent research in sociology; Polaroid snapshots of my father's face the night after his nose was broken in a bar brawl; graphic pages torn out of a porn magazine with handwritten captions identifying my father as one figure, my mother as another, and a woman with whom he had had an affair as a third. The letters themselves were predominantly loving and parental, but there was usually a paragraph or two in each that revealed his paranoid and delusional thought processes. I kept all of his letters and most of the enclosures, but seldom wrote back.

As soon as I saw it I knew I had found the letter I would read at the service. He had written it in 1986 on the occasion of my seventeenth birthday, during a period of relative stability when he was struggling to reclaim his past.

Dearest Nathaniel,

I have sent along a packet of materials which represents the bringing to a close of my research which will be completed in April. I thought I would spend the extra few dollars and buy the dream with dignity. It represents about 13 man months worth of work. I have done a mailing of 150 of those packets and that will be it. I will summarize the whole thing in 10 pages and mail it out with my résumé in the fall if I do not get a job this year. My strategy from now on is to write articles for professional publication only and this I will continue to pursue for as long as I keep going.

This is your birthday present and I wish you to learn only one lesson from it. No matter how adverse the circumstances—and mine have been adverse—there is never any reason to give up—

whether it is writing poetry or doing art—my
interests at the time—*or dabbling in highly eso-*
teric subjects such as I do. I do not even expect much
of a reaction to the mailing. Several letters of inter-
est and perhaps a job offer would suit me just fine.
But even if that does not materialize I will always
have the satisfaction of knowing that I have done
my best work and followed through. That is really
the most important thing.

You probably will receive this letter before the
materials since I could not afford to mail them first
class. Remember I remembered your birthday.

Love, Dad.

When I received that letter I did not understand the
adversities my father had faced because of his disorder—I only knew what I had endured as a result of his
onslaught of phone messages and correspondence—so
his lesson did not make the same impression on me that
it did after his death. Had I been more prescient at the
time, I might have applied my father's lesson to our
relationship and taken advantage of the apparent
renewed clarity of his thinking to try to rebuild what
we had had. I was not able, however, to put aside my
fear of him or his strange behavior.

Three years later, in 1989, in response to an emotion-
ally charged delusional letter from my father, I wrote
him a short note, cutting off all contact. My explanation was succinct: "I cannot live in your world; you can-

not live in mine." He continued to write to me from time to time, but it was not until five years later, on Christmas Day, 1994, that I finally responded, sending him as a Christmas present a copy of a children's book I had written. I wanted him to know that I had finally emerged on the other side of adolescence, albeit at the late age of twenty-five, and was ready to try again. I mailed it to Manchester, New Hampshire, which was the return address on one of his most recent letters to me. My father died one week later in Burlington, Vermont, without knowing that he was still in my thoughts.

As I read through the stack of letters, I discovered that I remembered the content of most of them. When I picked up the last envelope, however, I had no memory of it at all. The postmark was October 1992 and the return address was 16 Hickock Place, Burlington, Vermont. I was shocked. I realized that I *had* known that my father had moved from New Hampshire to Vermont; I had simply forgotten. If I had remembered his last letter, there might have been a chance that he would have received my present before he died.

To a mind woken up too late by death, my father's last letter was full of clues that he was entering a new, more desperate stage in his life. For the first time he addressed me as "Nat—" and signed the letter, simply, "Dad." Gone were the familiar terms of endearment: "Dearest Nathaniel," "Love, Dad." His handwriting had changed; his controlled, tiny hand had been replaced by a sloppy,

uneven scrawl that mirrored his psychological deterioration. He referenced an enclosure, a summary of his
recent work, but forgot to include it in the envelope.

Nat—

Thought you might be interested in the enclosed. I have
collapsed 20 years of work into 9 months by formaliz-
ing all of the intuitions based on "my experience."
Immediate need: $325.00. Exploring possibility of rais-
ing 250K. Initiatives under way for position or funding
from Australia to Saudi Arabia. Up for three local posi-
tions plus in contact with a Teacher Agency. With or
without this working out plan to be in Canada by
September. Have lost faith on the basis of this experi-
ence in this country to manage its affairs—can demon-
strate and prove it. Will wait to produce to hear from
marketplace. Spend the time in the library at
University of Vermont finishing research. Seeking a
lawyer to sue Manchester Mental Health. Have three
witnesses, credibility, one successful test and two others
possible. Cannot pin CIA or Pentagon or your mother.
If you have any interest in the enclosed let me know.

> *Dad*
> *16 Hickock Place*
> *Burlington, VT 05401*

PS Clifford has invested $300 and my former landlord
$1,500. Eating in so by January will have $250 to $300
discretionary.

My father's last letter to me was written in October 1992, five months before he became homeless. I did not understand the reference to Manchester Mental Health or his "test," but I did not need to in order to understand that the letter was an indirect entreaty for financial assistance. I wanted to convince myself that I only realized the point of the letter when I rediscovered it after his death. The truth was, however, that holding it in my hand again I distinctly recalled being surprised when I first read it that my father would ask his estranged son for money. Although I was then twenty-two years old, it did not occur to me that this in and of itself was an indication that he was in dire straits. I had become so comfortable with the idea of my father as an unpredictable and at times bizarre correspondent that I had lost all sense of the man, existing in real time, struggling to put his life back together. I let the letter go unanswered. My father never contacted me again.

The next morning at the funeral service I read aloud my father's advice to me on my seventeenth birthday: "No matter how adverse the circumstances—and mine have been adverse—there is never any reason to give up." He had heeded his own advice. The rejection letters from the colleges that the police officer found in my father's apartment proved that even after his transformation into the transient eight years later, my father was still trying to put his life back together, still trying to reclaim his past.

For my part, I did not learn the lesson in time. I gave

up on my father and our relationship while he was still alive. Although it was now too late, I decided to try to apply his lesson anyway. After all, if there really was never any reason to give up, then even death should not be a deterrent. After learning that my father had died *and* that he had been homeless the year before his death, I was determined not to turn my back on him again. I resolved to find out what had happened to him and why—to answer the question posed by the officer investigating my father's death: "How did he get to be in *this* apartment in *Burlington, Vermont?*"

It was the summer of 1995 and the word "transient" kept ringing in my ears, amplified by a growing sense of guilt about my having abandoned my father. I began to study him. I began to see beyond the uniform—the dirt, the hair, the beard—to see the individual permutations of the transient, and to see each of those permutations as a person. I began to distinguish between the young and the old, the newcomers and the perennials, the addicts and the mentally ill, and to wonder how each had undergone a similar transformation. I wanted to talk to them, to learn from them about my father's disorder and about his life on the street.

I was rebuffed by several—a middle-aged man from Oregon who lived in a cardboard box outside the Cuban embassy and believed that he had a direct telepathic link to Castro; a jaundiced, emaciated woman who was always teetering on the arm of a different male transient; a strikingly handsome, unkempt man in his twenties who stood on the same street corner every day, muttering profanity at passersby. Then, I met the Masked Rider, a middle-aged black man with broken teeth and a bad leg who had lived on stoops and in doorways in the Murray Hill section of Manhattan for more than a decade. I sat down next to him one morning and, after volunteering that my father had been homeless, asked him if it would be all right to ask him some questions. It was clear from the start that he wanted someone to talk to almost as much as I did. We quickly became friends and started having breakfast together every morning on the same brownstone stoop. Some days we went Dutch; some days I treated. On a few occasions, when he had money left over from the previous day's panhandling, he insisted on treating me.

Bit by bit, the Masked Rider told me about his past. He grew up in Philadelphia in the 1940s and moved to New York in the early 1960s to try to make it as a trumpet player. He sat in with some of the jazz greats, including Miles Davis and John Coltrane. His break came in 1965 when he played on Coltrane's seminal album, *Ascension*. By the late 1960s, however, something had gone wrong. He was sleeping on the floor in the basement of a bar in the East Village and spending his time putting together a collage book that consisted of words and phrases that he had cut out at random from discarded magazines. He was convinced that the book, which he named *Atomic Science* because "it sounded like something people would read," was worth millions, but explained that it was stolen from him before he could complete it. He had been homeless on and off ever since.

One morning, after finishing a miniature of Jack Daniel's, he revealed his true identity to me. The Masked Rider was a character from an old western serial he had loved as a boy. He could not explain how it happened, but sometime back in the 1980s he discovered that he had actually *become* the Masked Rider. He added in a secretive whisper that his wife was the Scarlet Horseman, a character from another western serial. He would not tell me her name, but said that she lived in the neighborhood and gave him a dollar every day on her way to work. They had never discussed their marriage openly, but the Masked Rider was certain that she knew they were husband and wife.

There was one subject the Masked Rider was more guarded about than any other—his father. When he finally felt comfortable enough with me to talk about him, I learned that we shared an unexpected bond: our fathers had, by their presence and their absence, defined who we were.

"I am only going to go a certain distance, but I will say this. I never knew my father. I never even saw him. He got stabbed, so he had to go to the funeral parlor.

But it is through *my father* that they have done this, hurt me this way. The way I knew was I was sitting around the corner one day, and it felt like somebody was cutting the nerve in my leg. It had to be that because nerves do not just collapse. They have cut from a high point in my hip all the way down my leg, down into my foot. All he has got to do is touch something and it really is painful. It seems like wherever that pain is, my father be right there. And he is not even here! That is really hard to figure out. My father's already in his grave, and he is doing this for these people to be in office. I do not know why they want to be in politics like that. To me, it is wrong. Very unfair. The President has got children, got a wife, and he has hurt everybody. Hurt me, hurt my family. God, we are barely hanging on, whoever is left, we are barely hanging on."

At least once every morning during our breakfast, the Masked Rider would take out a tiny spiral notebook, which he kept in his shirt pocket, and write down the numbers 1 through 7. When he finished explaining how the government had employed his father's ghost to keep him incapacitated and living on the street, for example, he filled an entire page with sequences of numbers. In part out of curiosity, in part to allow me time to digest what he had just said, I asked him what the numbers meant.

"I heard a long time ago seven was a significant number. Which means that it is one through seven that vibrates. So, if you come into a difficult moment, you can write that down, and it will change the vibration. And the number eleven—speak of death—that is death. Number eleven. You write that down, you done die. Seven, it could represent dying, too. If I have trouble going to the bathroom, or after I take a drink, or if I talk to somebody, I write it down. I usually try to count to seven, but I seem to be so advanced in it now that most of the time I do not have to go all the way. I get to about three, and it is done. But it is different with politics. Politics is bad right now."

The sacred symbols of his world almost made sense to me. Listening to him was like stepping off a remote island into a church for the first time. You stare blankly at Christ on the cross, the Virgin Mary, the pews, the candles, the altar. You sense that there is meaning in these objects, that this strange world is important to the people who constructed it, but you cannot connect it all. In the mind of every person suffering from schizophrenia there exists an entire city of thought which is inaccessible to anyone other than its architect.

The Masked Rider and I are still friends to this day and he is still living on the street. His bad leg has atrophied, but otherwise he is exactly the same. For a while I tried to help him change his situation. When he mentioned one morning that he still had siblings in Philadelphia, I tried to convince him to call them, but he told me that he did not want them to see him in his current condition. "Besides," he added cryptically, "there is trouble in the family." He refused to elaborate, but made it clear that he meant something other than his experiences with his father. When I suggested that he go to a shelter at night instead of sleeping in the subway, he told me that he would never go to one again because the last time he went an employee had complained about how bad he smelled. When I asked him if he would let me take him to the emergency room so he could have his leg examined, he explained that his problems are political and that if he can get the vibrations right, his father will leave him alone and he will be able "to get up and walk out of here." I never mention the issue of his mental health; he does not believe that he has a mental illness and refused to talk to me for a week the one time I broached the subject. In the end, I try to help him the way he helps me, by being there to listen.

When the Masked Rider told me that there was trouble in the family, it occurred to me for the first time that he might have children. His answer to my question, like most of the things he says, surprised me.

"The way I believe, the children are here. I am fifty-four years old. So I know they are here. But the way they were born, it was a different way. Basically, it is through the spirit that it happens. I do not know if you know this, but there is ten children in every family. Some people are lucky enough to get into bed and do the stuff. And in nine months the woman goes to the hospital and has a baby. But a lot of people cannot experience that. But the thing is if they really thought, they would know that they got children, too. It is just the way that they are here. What I am saying is that I am a human being. If something happened where I could not do that, somehow those children are here. I think about mine all the time."

I almost asked him an unforgivable question at that point in the conversation: did he resent his children for turning their backs on him, leaving him on the street to struggle with the government, his father's ghost, and his bad leg? But I could see from the expression on his face that he did not; his smile expressed his feelings of love and paternal pride more powerfully than any words could. It was time for both of us to start our day. Our breakfast that morning ended the way it always did. After shaking my hand, the Masked Rider tested his bad leg and headed in the direction of Park Avenue. He was going to meet his wife at Grand Central Station. With some luck, he would collect enough change to buy lunch and another miniature of Jack Daniel's to help shorten his day. As I watched him hobble slowly down the brownstone-lined street, commuters stepping around him without breaking their stride, hotels and high-rises in the distance, I found myself wondering what Burlington looked like, and tried to imagine what it would feel like to stand on Church Street—another American street which a transient had made his home.

Chapter 2

The
Outsider

It was not until I made my first pilgrimage to Burlington, Vermont, exactly one year after my father's death, that I knew for certain that the transient was not just an artifact of New York City life. Burlington, situated on the eastern shore of Lake Champlain, about ten miles west of the Green Mountains, is a center of regional tourism; its population, thirty-nine thousand, makes it the largest city in Vermont. Church Street, the street where my father panhandled and later died, is home to the Marketplace, Burlington's hub, a brick-paved pedestrian thoroughfare flanked by two rows of upscale shops, ending at the door of a white, steepled church. The Marketplace is a magnet for tourists taking a break from—depending on the season—boating on Lake Champlain, appreciating the autumn foliage, or schussing down the ski slopes. The Marketplace is also a magnet for the homeless, of whom there are estimated to be six thousand in the state. The constant flux of pedestrians and the park benches scattered all along its length provide transients with ample opportunity to panhandle, observe, and socialize.

Walking up Church Street for the first time in January 1996, surrounded by families wearing colorful parkas and toting skiing paraphernalia, I felt resentful that there was nothing to commemorate that this strip of rinky-dink stores was a battlefield—a twentieth-century Gettysburg or Appomattox. Here, a man had fought the greatest battle of all: the battle to preserve the dominion of the self against an invading cancer of the mind. I was abruptly reminded that the battle had not ended. On a park bench opposite Leunigs, an upscale bar and restaurant, an unkempt, bearded man was smoking a cigarette with trembling hands and muttering to himself. If passersby noticed him at all, it was with studied indifference. I resisted the temptation to sit next to him and ask about his father and vibrations and his ten children, although it was easy to imagine for a moment that all transients drew on the same pool of symbols and private meanings.

I continued up Church Street, trying without success to feel something specific and meaningful—trying, I suppose, to discover traces of my father. Deep in the pocket of my coat, my fingers found my favorite photograph—an old dog-eared snapshot of the two of us from the late 1970s. In the photograph, my father, confident and handsome, sits on a park bench. He is lighting his pipe, a trace of a smile on his lips. I am in the foreground, grinning at the camera, all teeth and elbows. More than any other photograph I had of the two of us, that image represented both what we lost and what we could have had.

At the mouth of Burlington Square Mall, a young man in his late twenties wearing stained army fatigues and a torn gray sweatshirt was talking animatedly to himself and gesticulating wildly. The flow of pedestrian traffic moved around him as if he were six times his actual size. When I walked past with the crowd, he noticed that I was looking at him. I could tell by the way he stiffened that I had unwittingly entered his battlefield. His reaction to me was so focused I felt like I had called out his name. I continued up the block, consciously restraining myself from turning back to see if he was still watching me. I heard my own voice telling me, "That could be you."

I was starting to become familiar with the Marketplace, starting to feel like I was a little closer to being on an equal footing with the locals. I had learned from the police officer who investigated my father's death that when he was living on the street he used to hang out at Leunigs. I stopped before reaching the church at the end of the street and made my way back there. At the bar I looked out through the floor-to-ceiling glass window that faces Church Street. The bearded transient was still sitting on the bench, and from this perspective I could see that he was watching the restaurant.

I turned and introduced myself to the bartender— the first of several portly, middle-aged men I would meet in Burlington who sported a walrus mustache. He had worked at Leunigs for seventeen years and had the bartender's habit of involving the regulars in all conversations. Ours was no exception. When I asked him if he remembered a customer named Charles Lachenmeyer, he told me he had never heard the name before, then asked the nearest regular if the name meant anything to him. The regular shook his head. I showed them both the photograph and described what my father might have looked like in the early 1990s. The bartender stared at me—my long face, my high forehead, my prominent chin—and suddenly remembered a man who used to frequent the bar whose name he never knew.

Leunigs was the first place on Church Street to open each morning and my father would come in at least a couple of times a week. When he first showed up, in the spring of 1993, he would sit at a table by the window for hours, staring out at Church Street and occasionally writing in a spiral notebook. He always ordered the same breakfast: eggs, coffee, and a couple of Budweisers. The bartender explained, "We have a rule: no alcohol in the morning. One of the reasons I think that he came in and got served was because he dressed more like a preppy than a carnie. It was not denim and leather and lots of tattoos; it was always chino pants and buck shoes and a sweater with an oxford collar shirt." From the outset the bartender suspected that my father might be homeless, but the way he dressed and the fact that he often paid by credit card left him unsure. As the weeks went by there was no longer any question that he was a transient. "His looks deteriorated the longer he sat there. When he started his hair was like mine, but by the end the hair was shaggy, the beard was shaggy, the fingernails were dirty."

The changes in my father's appearance made the waitresses uncomfortable, so the bartender started to encourage him to sit at the bar. Despite his evident isolation, my father never took advantage of the communal nature of the bar. "I never saw him interact with anybody." The bartender paused and shifted his body to include the regulars in what was clearly the start of one of his standard stories. "In all the time that he sat there, we only had one conversation to speak of. It was the only time I ever had to talk to him about his behavior. He was sitting at the bar and *talking to himself.* There were other people at the bar, people were uncomfortable with that, so I just went over and said, 'You will have to stop talking to yourself.' He said, 'I am not talking to myself, I am talking to my mother.' So I said, 'Be that as it may, talk to her without moving your lips.' And he *did.* He just stopped talking to himself. He was quiet, he finished his beer, and he left."

The bartender smiled and shrugged his shoulders, his story finished. The regulars at the bar managed one smile between them; they had heard the story before. I thanked him for his time and left. Not knowing where to go next, I sat down on the bench across the street—

the bearded transient had moved on—and looked at
Leunigs from his vantage point. It took me a few minutes to notice that it had started to snow. I pushed the
image of my father as a transient out of my mind and
began to think about the fact that he had heard his
mother's voice talking to him nearly twenty years after
her death. There could be no doubt that at the end of
his life my father was looking back into his past. The
police officer had found alumni directories in his apartment from the College of William and Mary, where he
went to college, and the Poly Preparatory Country Day
School in Brooklyn, where he went to high school. The
question was: what was he looking for? The alumni
directories could be explained easily enough: he was
casting a wide net for job opportunities and wanted to
contact people who had known him before all his trou-
bles began. This, however, did not explain his hearing
his mother's voice.

The snow stopped. Tourists strolled by in both directions, keeping a flock of local pigeons in flight over
Church Street with their voices and shuffling feet.
Leunigs filled up slowly with the lunch crowd. I tried to
see the scene through my father's eyes, but I could not.
Sitting on a park bench in the shadow of a small
steepled church, I realized that I had no way of understanding the sacred symbols of his world. Given that
one of the hallmark symptoms of schizophrenia is
auditory hallucinations, it was not surprising that he
was hearing voices and "talking to himself." But I could

not help asking myself what, if anything, was the significance of his auditory hallucination taking the form of his mother's voice.

Eventually, I gave up and headed back to my car. I realized that in order to understand my father's life as the transient, I needed to start, not in Burlington, Vermont, where he died, but in Brooklyn, New York, where he was born.

When I was growing up in Pelham, I spent as little time as possible in the basement of our house. If I was doing the laundry or getting my bike out, I would move as quickly as I could through its cold, partially finished rooms, my heart racing, my eyes skipping over the deep shadows left unexplored by the bare bulbs that were its only source of illumination. It was not just the dark that frightened me. The family cat had hidden there, waiting to die, after accidentally ingesting rat poison. From that point on I associated the basement with death. It made sense to me that when my grandfather died in 1979, that was where my father stored the suitcases containing his effects as well as the effects of my grandmother, who had died four years earlier.

The house is still in the family. The day after I returned from Burlington, I took the train to Pelham and searched the basement, looking for the suitcases. By the time I found them, stacked one on top of the other at the back of the closet next to my old board games, my hands were trembling; my old fear had returned. It intensified when I discovered two brown paper bags hidden in the space between the suitcases and the back wall. Inside each bag was an empty six-pack, still smelling faintly of beer. It amazed me to think that there was still evidence of my father's furtive drinking in the house so many years after he last set foot inside. Feeling like I had disturbed a gravesite, I returned the bags to their hiding place before rummaging through the suitcases.

Standing under a bare bulb, I read through old letters and address books, stared at photographs of relatives I could not identify, and examined my grandfather's mementos from World War II. The air around me grew heavy with dust and the smell of old people, reminding me of my grandparents' apartment in Bay Ridge, Brooklyn. An unfriendly place for a young boy, their home was cluttered with fragile bric-a-brac, there were plastic covers on all the furniture, and the television was always on too loud. My grandparents died before I could lock them in my memory. I recognized them from their photographs, but looking at their faces invoked in me nothing more specific than a general feeling of uneasiness, which seemed unrelated to my immediate surroundings.

I finished sorting through their effects, rounded up the address books and letters, and returned to Manhattan. Over the next few days I called every number in my grandparents' address books, but was unable to locate anyone who still remembered them. A trip to their old neighborhood in Bay Ridge and a series of advertisements in Brooklyn newspapers also yielded no results. I discovered that too much time had passed; Brooklyn had forgotten the Lachenmeyer family. There was only one person I knew of who could tell me about my father's life growing up: his first cousin, Clifford Eriksen, whom the police had called initially to notify that he had died. I had not seen Clifford since my parents' divorce fifteen years earlier, and was eager to meet him again, in part because he was the only family member who had stayed in contact with my father consistently after the onset of his disorder.

One week later I was sitting in Clifford's living room, examining his face to see what time had done to the family features. He looked very much the way I remembered him; he had the long face, the strong jaw, and the high forehead of all the men in our family. I had been uncomfortable around Clifford as a child, and now, as an adult, I understood why. His benevolent smile and calm, measured speech seemed more the result of profound self-control than a natural extension of his personality—an impression furthered by the tics that animated his face at regular intervals. Clifford and his brother, Joel, now deceased, were raised by my grandparents after their mother died when they were very young. As we discussed my father's upbringing, I found myself wondering what impact growing up in the Lachenmeyer family had had on Clifford.

My grandmother, Dorothea Kapps, was born in 1905 in Brooklyn, the youngest of three children. Dottie's father was a baker. Her mother claimed to be a descendant of German royalty, a count von Hinderer who sold his title in the 1800s after falling on hard times. Dottie began working as a secretary after graduating from high school. She had a pretty face, but was overweight and never bothered to have her unruly hair fixed, which gave her a somewhat harried, unkempt look. Her appearance was also marred by nervous tics, including an occasional clicking of her teeth.

By all accounts, Dottie was troubled; she was arrogant, unusually remote, and extremely suspicious of the motives of those around her. Summing up her social style, Clifford described a typical exchange with a neighbor that took place around 1950: "We were in the building going up to the apartment and someone turned to Dottie and asked, 'How are the boys today?' Dottie replied, 'What do you mean how are the boys today? Was there something wrong with them yesterday?' Dottie was very supersensitive."

My grandfather, William Lachenmeyer, was born to working-class parents in 1906 in a cold-water railroad flat in Greenpoint, Brooklyn. Bill was a short man with narrow shoulders, a large nose, and a winning smile, which he attributed to the Irish in him. After leaving school at fourteen, he found work as a day laborer. In 1932, the year he and Dottie were married, he began his forty-year career at "the B.U.G.," Brooklyn Union Gas. He spent fifteen of the next seventeen years attending night school, ultimately completing a master's degree in business administration. Bill's letters to Dottie during their courtship and later, during World War II, reveal him to be a passive man with an even disposition, a religious temperament, and a profound love for his wife.

It was not until ten years after they were married, in 1943, that Dottie and Bill's only child, Charles William Lachenmeyer, was born. At the time Dottie and Bill were living in a small one bedroom apartment in Bay Ridge, Brooklyn, within walking distance of Fort Hamilton and Fort Lafayette. Bill was thirty-seven and Dottie was thirty-eight. According to family lore, Dottie had a physiological condition that prevented her from having children, which was corrected when she had her appendix removed in the early 1940s. Dottie's attitude toward her son after his birth, however, suggests that her late pregnancy may have been unplanned and that rumors of her "condition" may have been a calculated attempt to minimize speculation that she did not want children—an unacceptable idea in those days.

Three months after Charles was born, Bill was drafted into World War II. Ostensibly to allow Dottie to continue to work, Charles began to live with her older sister, Frances, her husband, and their two sons, Clifford and Joel, who shared a one bedroom apartment in the same building. Dottie saw her son only at meals, which she ate in Frances' apartment. Surprisingly, this arrangement continued even after Bill's return from the war in October 1945. By this time Charles was calling Frances "Mommy," and Dottie by her first name. Evidently, Dottie had turned over the care of her son to her sister permanently.

Then, in 1947, the unexpected happened. Frances died of heart failure while still in her thirties. Her husband, an alcoholic who would disappear on benders for days at a time, vanished altogether. Dottie and Bill reclaimed Charles and took in Frances' two children, Clifford and Joel, who were ten and five years old, respectively, at the time. All five family members shared a small one bedroom apartment. Despite the radical change in their circumstances, Dottie continued to resist the role of motherhood. Dottie and Bill never legally adopted Clifford and Joel, and Dottie continued to encourage Charles to call her by her given name. This ambiguity made the interrelationships among the three boys difficult and confusing; their entire lives they would always refer to each other as "brother-cousins."

According to Clifford, Dottie's new familial obligations had a profound effect on her. "After never having been a mother, she was suddenly given three boys to raise. It was a great strain on her. In fact, there was a period of time, shortly after my mother's death, when Dottie stopped eating altogether. She lost so much weight that it appeared that she was going to die, too." In an attempt to cope with her sister's death and her new responsibilities, Dottie turned to a group that her sister had introduced to her shortly before she died— the Christian Science Church. She began attending services regularly after her sister's death, often bringing Charles, Clifford, and Joel with her. Bill remained a devout Catholic but did not object to her sudden conversion, apparently reassured by the superficial similarities between Catholicism and Christian Science. According to Clifford, still an ardent Christian Scientist to this day, "It was through Christian Science treatment that Dottie was healed."

The cornerstone of the Christian Science movement was laid in 1875 with the publication of a book called *Science and Health*, written by the movement's founder, Mary Baker Eddy. As expressed in *Science and Health*, the two main tenets of Christian Science are, first, that the material world does not exist independent of our perception of it; and, second, that our perception of the material world is a false belief—that is, a sin—which distracts us from living a moral life. Our bodies, our brains, the world around us, birth, and death—these are all false beliefs which prevent us from being at one with what Christian Science terms "the Divine Mind."

What makes Christian Science seductive is its claim that it can heal every sickness, stop aging, and even prevent natural death by teaching us that sickness, aging, and death do not exist. This is thought to be an effective method because the Christian Scientist believes that it is precisely the false belief in sickness, aging, and death that causes us to experience these phenomena. Christian Science anchors and legitimizes these claims by contending that the miracles described in the Bible are manifold examples of Christian Science at work, and that Jesus was, in fact, the first Christian Scientist.

There is a subtle invitation to arrogance and paranoia woven into the fabric of Christian Science that may have appealed to Dottie as much as the promise of miracles and kinship with Christ. Without examining in detail the strange life of the founder of Christian Science, Mary Baker Eddy, it is worth noting how she explained why even she, the "discoverer" of Christian Science and the self-proclaimed "Mother" of all Christian Scientists, showed all the normal signs of aging. She could not, of course, attribute it to a lack of faith, so she turned elsewhere, to other people and to what she termed "malicious animal magnetism." Animal magnetism, also known as mesmerism or hypnosis, was a competing school of alternative healing prevalent at the time Mary Baker Eddy was writing *Science and Health*. It was her belief that animal magnetism, the use of mental powers to exert a healing influence over another person, was neither positive nor benign.

The chapter "Animal Magnetism Unmasked," in the most recent edition of *Science and Health*, reveals this paranoia: "The mild forms of animal magnetism are disappearing, and its aggressive features are coming to the front. The looms of crime, hidden in the dark recesses of mortal thought, are every hour weaving webs more complicated and subtle. So secret are the present methods of animal magnetism that they ensnare the age into indolence, and produce the very apathy which the criminal desires." Mary Baker Eddy believed that malicious animal magnetism was capable of psychically damaging practitioners of Christian Science, of undermining their ability to heal themselves and others, and even of killing them; and that it was these "mental assassins" who were responsible for her own aging and ill health. She even blamed mental assassins for the death of her third husband, despite his physician's assertion that he died of heart failure. In a letter to the *Boston Post* published in 1882, she writes, "My husband's death was caused by malicious mesmerism . . . I know it was poison that killed him, not material poison, but mesmeric poison."

If Dottie was healed by Christian Science, it was not in the way that Clifford meant. Christian Science provided her with a socially acceptable framework for the expression of ideas that might otherwise have been viewed as symptoms of an emerging thought disorder. By redefining her aberrant personality traits as part of a system of religious belief, Dottie was able to escape most of the stress that would have resulted from her attempts to reconcile her behavior with the social expectations of her environment.

Dottie's belief in Christian Science extended far beyond a casual reading of *Science and Health.* It governed every aspect of her life after 1947 and exerted a profound influence over her family. Bill was insulated to some extent by his own faith, Catholicism, but the boys were urged at every stage in their development to supplant their perception of the world with an elaborate delusional system that systematically denied the reality of everything society as a whole teaches its children.

My father mentioned Christian Science to me only once when I was growing up. I had asked him why a friend's parents always insisted that I keep my elbows off the table whenever I ate dinner at their house. He explained that different parents believed different things and as a result had very different ways of raising their children. By way of illustration, he told me a story about what things were like for him as a kid. Once when he was a boy he fell and skinned his knee in front of Dottie. He was crying, but Dottie did nothing to comfort him; she just stared at him. Then, finally, she told him, "There is nothing wrong with you. Think that there is nothing wrong with you and the cut will disappear." My father's uncle, Freddie, heard him crying, came over, and cleaned out the cut. Dottie asked him not to interfere and kept saying to my father, "It will go away. Keep thinking that there is nothing wrong and it will go away." When I asked my father why his mother had not helped him, he said it was because she believed in something called Christian Science.

Unlike his brother-cousins, my father never accepted Christian Science. His stubbornness and independence of mind in the face of Dottie's incessant proselytizing guaranteed his isolation within the family. There was little relief from Christian Science for my father over the years. According to Clifford, "He was not involved in a lot of activity outside of the family as a child. We were a very tight knit family. There was very little opportunity for involvement in anything other than family activities." My father adapted by withdrawing and giving free reign to his imagination. As a young boy he would sit on the side of his bed for hours at a time with a sock on one hand and keep himself entertained, imagining that his hand was a knight engaged in battle. At P.S. 104 he told wild stories to shock and amuse his friends and teachers. Clifford remembered, for example, that "One of Charles' teachers was aghast at a story he told about a red mouse that he had and all the adventures they shared. The teacher just refused to believe the story. He actually did. It was a rubber mouse."

My childhood conversation with my father about Christian Science kept running through my head as Clifford and I danced around the subject and the effect it had on my father. I was starting to understand that my father's childhood had been profoundly influenced by his mother's belief system. I was also beginning to suspect that its influence had something to do with why my father heard his mother's voice in Burlington so long after her death. Sitting across from a true believer, I was unable to bring any of this up directly. Before Clifford and I parted company, however, I did ask him what he thought explained my father's outcome. It did not surprise me that he attributed what happened to personal failure—a combination of arrogance and alcohol—and that he had tried several times over the years to help my father rediscover the Christian Science faith. He believed until the very end that Christian Science could have healed him.

The highlights of my father's childhood were the summers. Each summer the Lachenmeyer family left Brooklyn for a few weeks and joined forces with Dottie's brother, Freddie, and his family at a converted boardinghouse he had inherited near Greenwood Lake in the Catskills. At the end of our conversation, Clifford suggested that I call Freddie's granddaughter Marilyn—whom I had never heard of before—to learn more about my father's experiences at Greenwood Lake. I called her as soon as I arrived home. I was eager to ask her about her memories of my father's childhood, in part because I knew that her branch of the family had escaped the pull of Christian Science.

I assumed that she and my father had been out of touch since they were kids, but she told me that he had called her out of the blue in 1986, after being out of contact for more than twenty-five years. They spent the entire conversation reminiscing about Greenwood Lake—how they swam each morning before breakfast and every afternoon sat perched on a hill, staring at mountains that seemed far away to young eyes; how when he was twelve and she was nine they shared a first kiss behind a bungalow before being chased into the open by a swarm of bees. Three decades fell away in an instant when they recalled the scene. They could not stop laughing when they remembered how the family covered them with mud to keep the swelling down. Their laughter reminded Marilyn of the boy she had fallen in love with as a young girl.

The summers at Greenwood Lake represented Charles' first opportunity to step out of the shadow cast by his family. Every year at Greenwood Lake, Charles seemed to find and befriend a new stray dog, which became his loyal companion for the summer. He loved to explore the woods around the lake with the dog at his side. Often, Marilyn joined them on their adventures. Charles knew all about the woods—the names of trees and rocks, the history of every fossil he found—and loved to act as Marilyn's guide. According to Marilyn, he would become more and more happy and relaxed the farther they were from the boardinghouse. "He was very different from his cousins and his parents. He was so kind and full of energy, and he was a little bit more of a thinker than the rest of us. I remember one day we were sitting up on the hill. It must have been one of our last summers there. I asked him what he liked best about being at Greenwood Lake. He told me that he liked being outside; and then he said that he guessed that made him an outsider. I always remembered him saying that because I thought of him that way. An outsider. It was like he was a stranger in his own family."

After their telephone conversation in 1986, Charles began to call Marilyn once or twice a year. She sensed that things were not going well for him when he continued to keep their conversations firmly rooted in the past. Sensing that he was unhappy and lonely, she also found herself wondering if he was an alcoholic; there were many in the family. One of their last conversations confirmed her suspicions. It was apparent from Charles' voice that he had a cold, and when Marilyn admonished him to eat well he replied that all he had in the refrigerator was beer.

Marilyn never suspected that anything else was wrong with Charles until their last conversation, in January 1993, two months before he became homeless. At the end of that conversation it suddenly became clear to Marilyn that Charles was crazy. "For some reason it was like he wanted to give me something, like I deserved to get something from him. I said, 'What are you talking about?' And he said, 'Well, would you like to meet the President?' I said, 'What do you mean,

Charles?' And he said, 'Well, you know, I could have him fly down and meet you. I would love him to meet you. Would you like to meet him?' I tried to say that the President might be too busy, but he kept going on and on like that. At the end of the conversation, he promised to call again. He never did."

Later that night I mulled over the new evidence that my father had been reaching into the past in the months leading up to his becoming homeless. It seemed less and less likely that his hearing his mother's voice twenty years after her death was an arbitrary phenomenon. I wondered what he felt when he and Marilyn reminisced about Greenwood Lake—a time before time, when he still had a future. Recalling his statements about the President, I also wondered whether it was a coincidence that he had abandoned a delusional system tinged with paranoia and delusions of grandeur in his youth only to embrace another, much more idiosyncratic one later in life.

After attending P.S. 104 for nine years, in 1957 my father applied for and received a full scholarship from the Poly Preparatory Country Day School, an exclusive private school located in Bay Ridge. In the spring of 1996 I attended the thirty-fifth reunion of his high school class. Generously outfitted with a name tag and a thirty-fifth reunion baseball cap, I spent the afternoon wandering around campus, under cherry blossoms and over sprawling lawns, talking to anyone who was similarly adorned. My father's classmates had been briefed by the school about my attendance and were accommodating, although it was clear that my presence was at cross-purposes with their nostalgia.

Poly Prep offered Charles a chance to test his intellectual mettle. He took to academics immediately and was an exceptional student, but he retained the sense that he was an outsider. One classmate, for example, who had also been a scholarship student, remembered, "Charles and I often talked about the fact that we were public school kids coming into a school with kids who were much wealthier than we were. So for a time it was 'us' and 'them.' I think Charles enjoyed doing so well, not only because it was important to do well academically, but because it was in effect beating them at their own game." Evidently, Charles had grown accustomed to feeling removed from his environment and different from the people around him. He did not try to fit in at Poly Prep; if anything, he drew sustenance from being the outsider.

High school provided Charles with his first real sense that there existed a world that did not depend upon the teachings of Mary Baker Eddy for its definition of reality. He reveled in his newfound freedom. For the first time, he was not asked to relinquish his emerging ideas and beliefs, only to study hard and demonstrate his ability to learn. Thus encouraged, Charles began to examine his family and their beliefs with a critical eye. At a time when the social sciences were not taught in high school, he spent his free time in the library, reading every book he could find on psychology and sociology that dealt with family. In his effort to analyze the dynamics of his family members' interaction and reduce his vulnerability to them, Charles became a nascent social theorist.

After my trip to Burlington I began to read through all of my father's early academic writing—published and unpublished—which I found in a file cabinet in the basement of the house in Pelham. I discovered that in graduate school he had written a book-length manu-script entitled *Explaining Human Behavior*, in which he grappled with the inadequacies of contemporary research methodology in sociology. One passage in par-ticular provides insight into his attempt as a teenager to understand what was wrong with his family. Discussing ways of testing the validity of explanations of social behavior under conditions in which the theorist is not only a researcher but a participant, he used the follow-ing example.

"Suppose you are the son of demanding, difficult parents. You have known this for some years, but have been willing to sacrifice because you assumed that your parents would still do anything for you. However, from little incidents here and there you begin to suspect that your parents are totally selfish: they ask sacrifices of you, but are not willing to make sacrifices for you. You decide to test this explanatory statement by producing a set of social behavioral sequences in which there are costs to your parents and rewards to you. Suppose, for example, that every Christmas your oldest brother, his wife, and their children come to stay at your parents' house. Every Christmas you have willingly let them have your room and slept on the floor for the five day interim. You decide this Christmas to test your prediction, so you refuse to give up your room or sleep on the floor. You then observe your parents' reactions. You hope that your parents will acquiesce and send your oldest brother and his family to the nearest hotel—with some hesitation no doubt, but that they will still give in. If your prediction is correct, however, your parents will become more demanding than ever and meet every one of your refusals with more intense demands. They will never back down and will bring all their pressure to bear to force you to give in. As a theorist it is your decision as to the degree of testing and confirmation you will be satisfied with."

Reading this passage, there can be little doubt that Charles conducted exactly this experiment as a teenager and that Clifford, who was married with two children when Charles was still living at home, is the hypothetical oldest brother. Charles concludes, "The theorist must control his own actions according to his predictions in order to test these predictions. This, in turn, necessitates that he be willing to and capable of changing his actions and reactions at a moment's notice—a requirement not easily met by normal men."

This somewhat self-aggrandizing statement contains a lot of truth, perhaps more than was intended. Charles was, of course, using "normal" in the sense of "average" rather than as the opposite of "*abnormal.*" But the fact remains that it is abnormal behavior to use one's own family as scientific subjects. His having conducted these "tests" does not mean that Charles was himself abnormal; the "tests" were a creative response by a very intelligent boy to difficult circumstances. There is, however, a disturbing potential for confusion and stress entailed in the act of treating one's daily interactions as a series of extended experiments, as games governed by rules that one must keep hidden from the people with whom one is interacting. This is all the more true when one is conducting these experiments with one's own family.

Reflecting his growing distance from his family, Charles did not return to Greenwood Lake the summer after his junior year at Poly Prep. Instead, he got a job as a dishwasher at the Wassakeag School, a study camp for boys situated on the shores of a lake near Dexter, Maine, a town with a population of five thousand in the center of the state. Clifford and Charles' classmates at Poly Prep both recalled that Charles was different when he returned to Brooklyn at the end of the summer.

Working in Dexter was a transformational experience for Charles. In the evenings he drove into Dexter and hung out on stoops, rubbing shoulders with the town's unemployed. The men he met were tough, independent, and a little dangerous. It was while sitting on those stoops that Charles first heard someone openly mock Christian Science. It was also while sitting on those stoops that he discovered his fondness for alcohol. Both experiences gave Charles his first taste of rebellion. Dottie did not drink and did not approve of alcohol, and he knew that she also would not have approved of his associating with men so far removed from the Christian Science ideal. In Dexter, Charles discovered a world distinct from Poly Prep and the future that studying hard in school promised, a world that reminded him of Bay Ridge and his working-class roots but that was not tainted by Christian Science or his family's insularity. For the first time he found a place where he could be an outsider without being alone. He was handed a beer and welcomed as an outcast among outcasts.

Charles' sense of identification with the men he met in Dexter did not prevent him from excelling academically his senior year at Poly Prep. After being offered a full scholarship, he decided to attend the College of William and Mary in Williamsburg, Virginia, that fall, following in the footsteps of both Joel and Clifford before him. He graduated from Poly Prep in June 1961. That summer he again worked at the Wassakeag School. Sitting around in the evening in Dexter, a beer in hand, Charles was happier than he had ever been. He was ecstatic at the prospect of leaving Brooklyn and his family behind. He had every reason to believe that the future was his to claim.

Chapter 3

The
Gatekeeper

During the summer of 1996 I sent letters to all of my father's former classmates from the College of William and Mary, using an alumni directory similar to the one the police officer had found in my father's apartment at the time of his death. The number of phone calls and letters I received over the next few months surprised me. Discovering how long the memory of someone can live, dormant, in so many people's minds reminded me of something my father had written in one of his delusional pamphlets, reflecting on his own parents' deaths: "We all leave behind memories as our primary legacy."

A composite image of my father slowly emerged from his classmates' recollections: at eighteen he had a heavy Brooklyn accent, a sharp wit, a way with logic, and an eye for bullshit. He was tall and athletic with a strong jaw and an imposing presence. Always animated when he spoke, he had an impressive vocabulary in both directions—cultured and profane—and never slowed down to accommodate the pace of Williamsburg. Although the person they remembered did sound a little like my father—if you allowed for the loss of his Brooklyn accent—I related best to an image several classmates described with a smile I could see even over the telephone: my father walking briskly to class every morning with a campus mutt he had befriended fast on his heels, both oblivious to everything around them.

Classmates who knew Charles as a casual acquaintance described him as very bright, self-confident, self-possessed, and a character. The few who got to know him better saw bravado in his volatile mixture of rigorous academic and self-conscious street tough. Brian Chabot, Charles' roommate for three years at William and Mary, was in a unique position to witness the contrast between his public and private personas. "He developed this attitude about being tough, about being sure of himself, that was very different from who he was in more private moments. When people were around he would tell stories about drinking and 'the neighborhood,' and sometimes even try, I think, to intimidate people physically by the way he acted. But he was also a very intelligent, very intellectual person. He seemed most comfortable when he was talking about ideas. That was when his tough guy stance would fade a little and he would become more relaxed."

At eighteen, Charles was trapped in the divide between his unusual upbringing and the new world he hoped to conquer. By the time he arrived at William and Mary he had rejected Christian Science and his family. He was not able to reject completely, however, the cumulative impact of eighteen years of mixed messages, of being taught over and over again to doubt his perceptions and beliefs. In his effort to establish an identity for himself and to cope with the social stresses of college life, he began to replace his personal history with a more romantic, fictitious past. He capitalized on the cultural distinction of being a Brooklynite in the genteel South and on his experiences in Dexter, Maine, to create the persona of the proverbial outsider—the New York kid from the mean streets. Charles completed the public image of himself with the aid of alcohol, which served as a prop and as another way of dealing with his insecurity. Chabot recalled, "He definitely consumed more alcohol than most of the rest of us did. I remember he had an affection for cheap wines. He would pick up a bottle of Thunderbird and joke about it, but it would be part of his weekend."

Charles never allowed his new persona or his taste for alcohol, however, to compete with his academic aspirations. He continued to be preoccupied with understanding his family's dynamics, and to look to the social sciences for answers. After dispensing with most of his general course requirements his freshman year, Charles took classes in psychology, sociology, and philosophy his sophomore year. With the encouragement of his professors, he decided to major in sociology,

defined in the course description of his introductory
class as "the study of the history, development, organization, and problems of people living together as social
groups." His minor was social psychology. In the years
before grade inflation, he received A's in every sociology
course he took in college. He had found his calling.

In the fall of 1996 I visited Williamsburg to learn more
about my father's interest in sociology from two of his
former professors at William and Mary. Colonial
Williamsburg, the large-scale re-creation of Colonial
life dedicated to the belief "that the future may learn
from the past," dominates the town of Williamsburg,
creating a surreal environment where the eighteenth
and twentieth centuries compete for attention in a marriage of history and commercialism. As I walked down
Duke of Gloucester Street, planning the questions I
would ask, an actor in period costume confronted me
with an archaic greeting and a theatrical bow. This
invitation to participate in his conflation of the past and
present reminded me of Church Street, where a transient had invited me into his delusional world with a
similarly misdirected look of recognition.

Without returning his greeting, I turned around and
headed in the direction of the college. The eighteenth
century also loomed large on campus. The quadrangles
were decorated with revolutionary war cannons, imposing statues, and an endless array of commemorative
plaques. As I wandered across the quadrangles I discov-

ered without trying to that Thomas Jefferson, James Monroe, and John Marshall were all alumni of William and Mary. The preservation of the past seemed to inoculate William and Mary against the passage of time. Although the number of students at the college had tripled to 7,500 students, things could not have looked much different when my father entered William and Mary as a freshman in 1961. I half expected to run into him on one of the quadrangles, involved in a heated debate about one of the big books of the day—David Reisman's *The Lonely Crowd* or C. Wright Mill's *The Power Elite*.

The day I arrived in Williamsburg, Dr. Wayne Kernodle, chairman of the sociology department at William and Mary during the early 1960s, since retired, welcomed me into his home. An octogenarian with an unvarnished Southern accent and a vitality that belied his age, Dr. Kernodle shook my hand firmly, then introduced me to his colleague, Dr. Edwin Rhyne, a fellow Southerner who had also taught my father at William and Mary. Once we were seated, Dr. Kernodle asked me with a smile if I remembered meeting him. When I shook my head, he laughed and explained that we had met once before in 1973 when my father, my mother, and I visited Colonial Williamsburg on a vacation. I had no recollection of the trip—I was four years old—but I had twin photos of my father and me in tacky Colonial hats to prove that it did take place.

Dr. Kernodle remembered the visit well. "My wife

and I were sitting in the house. The doorbell rang and I went to the door and saw this big tall guy. He said, 'You probably do not remember who I am.' I said, 'Come in, Charles.' He said, 'Well, I brought my wife and son with me.' You all came in and visited for a while. We had a good conversation. Charles was doing well then, teaching in New York, publishing quite a bit—he had just had his second book published by the Free Press. I remember thinking he looked good. Grown up."

My father also stopped by Dr. Rhyne's office when he visited Williamsburg with my mother and me. A generation younger than Dr. Kernodle, Dr. Rhyne was still on the faculty. He touched the bow tie he wore on days when he had class, and smiled at the memory. "It was obvious that he felt good about his life. He and his wife seemed happy and he was very proud of his little tyke who was tumbling all around. He was clearly saying, 'This is my boy.' He was also very excited about his work. It was clear that he had hit the ground running and was making a name for himself."

Dr. Kernodle first had Charles as a student in the spring of 1961, and was immediately impressed with the freshman from Brooklyn, New York. "He was brilliant—one of the best students that we have ever had in sociology, and one of the best students that William and Mary has ever had." Over the next three years Charles met with Dr. Kernodle frequently during his office hours to debate the issues of the day. Dr. Kernodle was especially taken with his willingness to engage in critical exchange and to take intellectual risks. Grinning appreciatively, he remembered, "He would not just take it. He would argue." The smile on Dr. Kernodle's face jumped to Dr. Rhyne's. "Charles was definitely a question asker. He was also a question *answerer*, and it is hard to say which he took more pleasure in. His great strength, however, was the clarity and originality of his mind. Charles was not only one of the brightest, quickest students that I have been privileged to have; he was also one of the most distinctive. He looked on the world with a slightly different vision from most people."

Listening to Dr. Kernodle and Dr. Rhyne's description of their former student made me forget Burlington and the intervening years and see my father as they had seen him: a gifted young man with unlimited potential. I knew from my own experience growing up in the shadow of my father's delusional system what had given him his different vision—being raised as a Christian Scientist.

When a parent presents a child with a way of looking at the world that contradicts his direct experience of reality, that child has two choices: accept the parent's perspective or come to terms at an early age with one of the most important lessons there is in life—reality is created as well as discovered. There is no other way to explain, for example, how an individual can read a book and become so convinced that all her experiences of the

physical world are false beliefs reflecting her own sin-
fulness that she devotes herself to converting whom-
ever she can to her point of view. A child who comes to
recognize that their parent's thinking is the product of
fixed delusions learns that the beliefs we hold most
sacred—the immutability of our physical and social
worlds; the immutability of our sense of self—are
expressions of faith, not of fact, and that nothing can be
taken as given in life.

Dr. Kernodle and Dr. Rhyne were the first people to
encourage Charles and to give shape and direction to
the skepticism his perspective entailed. They recognized quickly that he had a gift, a critical faculty that
owed its existence to no particular school of thought.
Most of the brightest students at any college in any
decade passively embrace the current, fashionable theory in their respective discipline. Their intelligence is
evidenced, not by their ability to critique and analyze
current trends in their chosen field, but by the energy
with which they assimilate and extend current thinking. Charles, however, was from the start very critical of
the field of sociology, even as he embraced its potential
and its appeal.

In the introduction to his first book, *The Language of
Sociology*, published by Columbia University Press in
1971, Charles summed up his perspective at the time:
"As an undergraduate major in sociology I felt a vague
intellectual strain in trying to make sociology relevant
to the things I observed around me. While stimulated
by the 'greats,' I remember being puzzled by sociology's

lack of power to explain the observable behavior of men. In my day-to-day affairs I would try to apply the general concepts I had inculcated, but to no avail: every explanation engendered a counter-explanation, every concept a rival."

By the beginning of his senior year, Charles had decided to apply to Ph.D. programs in sociology. In his senior thesis, which he completed in the fall of 1964, Charles gave an indication of the direction in which he was heading as a future sociologist. "Science demands of man the construction of theories and models of reality. Although these are meant to aid in his quest for knowledge, they may result in rigidified thought and defeat their ultimate purpose. They may be accepted as the only correct way of viewing events and become blinders guiding man past the truth. These thought traps are the most devastating and subtle for man." In order to maintain the flexibility of thought that is essential to the expansion of human knowledge, "theories and models must be not only filters through which reality is sifted but also objects of study in their own right. Above all, they must never be taken as the only valid approach to the truth or mistaken as a necessary adjunct to thought."

Charles saw himself as an intellectual gatekeeper, someone who could stop the horse of progress, pull its blinders off, and show the animal that it had options; that it was being driven down a particular path by a particular set of assumptions, and that these assumptions, being assumptions, could be altered at will, and a different, perhaps more rewarding path taken. He hoped to convert the different vision growing up with Christian Science had imposed on him into an avocation, an avocation that depended entirely on the continued clarity of his mind.

Charles worked hard and did well, receiving straight A's his senior year at William and Mary. This was an unusual enough occurrence at the college that the registrar delayed sending his transcripts to graduate schools because they assumed there had been a clerical error. He was accepted by his first-choice graduate school, Dr. Kernodle's alma mater, the University of North Carolina at Chapel Hill, and received a National Institute of Mental Health Four Year Fellowship in Social Psychology, which made it possible for him to attend. That spring, prior to graduation, Charles was initiated as a member of Phi Beta Kappa, the oldest and most prestigious Greek-letter fraternity in America, founded in 1776 at the College of William and Mary.

I brought with me to Williamsburg a handwritten journal which had the words, "Observations on a Closed Ward, Also Sundry and Diverse Thoughts by Charles Lachenmeyer," printed in block letters on the title page. I had found it by accident soon after my parents' divorce on a bookshelf in our house in Pelham, alongside my father's collection of books on sociology. The journal was dated 1964 and described my father's experiences working as an attendant at a state psychiatric hospital. I kept it, and although I had no idea where my father had written it, I was struck even then by the irony that he had worked with the mentally ill so many years prior to becoming ill himself. When I began to piece together the chronology of his life after I returned from Burlington, I realized that he must have worked at a psychiatric hospital while he was an undergraduate at the College of William and Mary.

When I showed the journal to Dr. Kernodle and Dr. Rhyne, they were able to confirm that during his senior year at William and Mary, my father had been an attendant at nearby Eastern State Hospital. A public institution located in Williamsburg, it was founded in 1770 "to make Provision for the support and maintenance of ideots, lunatics, and other persons of unsound minds." Eastern State Hospital marked his first introduction, outside of books and professional articles, to schizophrenia. In 1964, approximately three-fourths of the more than two thousand patients at Eastern State Hospital were diagnosed with schizophrenia.

Working as an attendant at Eastern State Hospital was not just a job for Charles; it was clear from his first journal entry that he saw Eastern State Hospital as an opportunity to apply the ideas in his senior thesis to the patients, the attendants, and the ward as a whole. "My goal: to develop a new point of view toward mental illness. Every innovation is the result of the assumption of a new point of view. Must break out of and stand outside of a system of thought before a new system can be developed." Based on the evidence of the journal,

Charles did not accomplish his goal while at Eastern State Hospital. The rest of the journal describes the daily life of patients in a state hospital in the mid-1960s. The tone of the entries is evenhanded, detached, and inquisitive:

"November 3, 1964. Much interaction between patients revolves around lighting cigarettes for each other with already lit cigarettes. (Patients are not allowed to carry matches.) At one point preference was shown to this form of lighting rather than my matches although I was right at hand with a match ready. An example here of the effects on social interaction of extrinsic structuring of the group.

"December 2, 1964. The impression is that patients have nothing with which to occupy their time, thus they aimlessly shift about. TV is the only regular activity provided, but it is not as much of a focal point for activity as would be expected. Head nurse says patients cannot concentrate, but it could also be a question of not concentrating because TV is the only thing there is to concentrate on."

In his self-appointed dual role of employee and researcher, Charles tried to earn the trust of the patients. While other attendants worked hard to maintain as much distance as possible between themselves and patients, Charles actually socialized with outpatients who lived in subsidized housing nearby. Several entries near the end of the journal refer to his staying up all night drinking and talking with the patients in their apartments. He no doubt saw this as a unique opportunity to build rapport with the patients and to observe them outside a controlled hospital setting; it was, in other words, part of his attempt "to develop a new point of view toward mental illness." But the fact that he got drunk with them suggested that something else was also at work: Charles identified with the patients. Hanging out with the patients, a beer in hand, Charles had discovered another Dexter, Maine, in the middle of the picturesque South. He had recovered the feeling of being an outsider among outsiders.

Struck by the apparent incongruence between Brian Chabot's characterization of my father, which seemed to be underscored by his journal entries, and his former professors' more hopeful recollections, I asked them a final question: what did they think the future held for my father? Looking back after thirty years, Dr. Kernodle and Dr. Rhyne both agreed that there was nothing in his behavior at William and Mary to suggest the course his life would take. In fact, they had hoped that he might eventually become one of the leading lights in sociology. They did, however, have the shared sense that he was prey to a fundamental insecurity that left him more vulnerable than he let on. According to Dr. Rhyne, "On the surface at least Charles knew what he was doing, knew what he thought, knew what he believed, knew where he was going. This was part of the picture that I think he liked to have of himself of being someone who knew what the rough-and-tumble of life was like and was perfectly capable of handling it all. But I always had the feeling that there was more self-doubt in him than he would admit and that at times he thought that he was not pulling off all that he wanted to accomplish."

The class of 1965's Senior Class Farewell in the College of William and Mary yearbook would prove to be, in my father's case, more accurate than maudlin. "Now we must leave, although not without regret. Here we have spent thirty-two months of our lives—a long time. We have learned many things and forgotten many others. We have made some friends and perhaps we have fallen in love. We have criticized many practices while we formulated a value system. Here in a word, we have had a home. Even the most rational and unsentimental among us must admit that the time and the place will never be recaptured."

Chapter 4

The
Sociologist

Charles reinvented himself prior to his arrival at the University of North Carolina at Chapel Hill in the fall of 1965. He returned his heavy Brooklyn accent to the prop room of adolescence and with it all of his sophomoric posturing about being a tough kid from the mean streets. He was a promising Ph.D. candidate in sociology from New York City, and that was how he wanted to be seen. The study of the history, development, organization, and problems of people living together as social groups presupposed a fluency in strategies of social interaction, which he worked hard to manifest. The one prop Charles was not able to dispense with, however, was alcohol; he was drinking enough by then to qualify as an alcoholic.

That winter Charles met and fell in love with the woman who would later become his wife—my mother—Julie Rasic, a fellow New Yorker and graduate student in the sociology department. Photographs of

Charles and Julie from that time show a young, happy couple in love. The backdrop in most of the pictures is a converted chicken coop just outside Chapel Hill, which Charles had rented and fixed up as a house. When the pictures are not of the two of them, arm in arm, Julie is usually the photographer and Charles is usually the subject: lifting weights in the backyard, completing his morning run, dropping a lobster into a pot, or sitting at his desk, surrounded by books.

For the first time, Charles talked openly about his past. Other than his experiences at Greenwood Lake, the only parts of his youth he described to Julie with evident pleasure were his two summers in Dexter, Maine. To him, Brooklyn was synonymous with his family, whom he had fought tooth and nail to escape. Charles was candid about his parents: his father was passive and ineffectual; his mother, manipulative, controlling, and paranoid. He detested Christian Science, calling it a dangerous denial and distortion of reality.

That distortion of reality was evident when Charles introduced Julie to his parents in early 1967. When Julie coughed at one point during dinner, Dottie leaned over and whispered in her ear, "Who are you resenting?" Julie suddenly understood what it would have been like to have grown up with Dottie as a mother. In an environment where every physical and psychological complaint was believed to be evidence of spiritual weakness—where nothing was ever what it seemed to be and the worst possible intention was assigned to every act—one could never be sure how to interpret one's own experiences.

The more Charles talked about his past, the more clear it became to Julie how preoccupied he was with the influence his family had had on his thinking and development. He had good reason: his mother's distortions of reality—her faith in Christian Science and her paranoia—had already come back to haunt him at the age of twenty-two. "Charles spent so much of his time fighting his mother and blaming her and seeing her as crazy and trying to control him," Julie remembered. "And yet he was also *like* her. He could get paranoid and he could be very manipulative, especially when he drank, and he would often interpret what someone else was doing as manipulating him, I think, because of her." Too often, and always with the aid of alcohol, the past broke through Charles' otherwise rational thought processes.

One bizarre incident that took place seventeen years before Charles was first diagnosed with schizophrenia suggests the extent to which his upbringing had interfered with his ability to accurately perceive the meaning of different social situations. One evening, Julie surprised Charles by making a new dessert. "I did not know it at the time, but it was Lent. Although we had never had any arguments or serious discussions about religious faith, Charles got very angry, assuming that I had made something new during Lent as a way to try to get him to be religious." Not only was he misinterpreting the situation, he was specifically interpreting it, in the absence of any evidence, as an attempt to make him religious—an indication of the impact of his mother's efforts to force him to see the world through the eyes of Christian Science.

Julie wrestled with the idea of breaking up with Charles, but he always apologized for his behavior and promised to cut back on his drinking. After meeting his parents, she thought she understood what was behind his erratic behavior and decided to try to make the relationship work. "I looked at his family and thought, God, if I grew up with them I would not know what was real either." Although Charles never discussed his aberrant behavior, independent of his drinking, it was clear that he too saw a connection between his mother, Christian Science, and his emerging personality problems. He devoted himself to understanding that connection in his master's thesis, entitled, "An Experimental Test of a Theoretical Model Deduced From the Double-Bind Hypothesis," which he completed in early 1968.

The double-bind theory was, in the mid-sixties, the dominant theory explaining the causes of schizophrenia. The theory, developed by Gregory Bateson, Don D. Jackson, and John H. Weakland and outlined in their article, *Toward a Theory of Schizophrenia*, argues that schizophrenia develops as a result of a specific type of sustained family interaction which they christen the "double bind." The double bind is "a situation in which no matter what a person does he 'can't win.'" The double-bind family interaction has these characteristics: a command by the parent directed at the child telling him not to do something or he will be punished; a simultaneous indication by the parent, whether explicit or implicit, that if the child obeys the command, he will also be punished; at the same time, the child is forbidden to comment on or escape the situation. The authors argue that with repeated exposure to the double bind, the child will learn to perceive his universe in double-bind patterns, resulting in an inability to accurately interpret any kind of interpersonal communication. The child's efforts to cope with this deficit ultimately result in what we call schizophrenia.

In their article, the authors cite this example of a double bind: "A young man who had fairly well recovered from an acute schizophrenic episode was visited in the hospital by his mother. He was glad to see her and impulsively put his arm around her shoulders, whereupon she stiffened. He withdrew his arm and she asked, 'Don't you love me anymore?' He then blushed, and she said, 'Dear, you must not be so easily embarrassed and afraid of your feelings.' The patient was able to stay with her only a few minutes more, and following her departure he assaulted an aide and was put in the tubs." The use of a mother-child relationship in this example is not arbitrary; the authors claim that it is usually the mother who instigates the double bind, while the father more often passively encourages the situation by refusing to support the child in his effort to break free from the double bind.

Charles' interest in the double-bind theory was entirely personal. "The reason he worked on the double bind was because he believed he had been raised in it," Julie remembered. "He related it very specifically to his mother and her treatment of him growing up. In his thesis he was trying to operationalize and measure in the short-run the situation in which he felt he grew up." Charles' assessment of his upbringing seems to be accurate. The incident in which he skinned his knee as a boy was a classic example of a double bind. In response to her son's cries, Dottie instructed him to apply Christian Science teachings and force himself to believe that he had not been hurt. She promised him that if he complied with her command, the cut would disappear. At the same time, it was understood that if he did not, he would be punished with her rejection of him. Irrespective of what he believed, however, the cut would not, of course, instantly heal; and the fact that it would not heal would indicate to his mother, as per Mary Baker Eddy, that he had not *really* accepted her command. In other words, whether or not he complied, he would be punished with her rejection. To make matters worse, he had no opportunity to escape or comment on the pattern of interaction because his father passively accepted Dottie's efforts to teach him Christian

Science, and because both of his brother-cousins were also ardent Christian Scientists.

The double-bind theory is no longer widely accepted as an explanation for what causes schizophrenia. Although there are several competing current theories, most researchers are in agreement that schizophrenia is caused by an interaction of neurological and environmental factors. Putting aside the issue of whether the double-bind theory has any generalized validity with respect to the development of schizophrenia, there is a lot of research—including Charles' dissertation—to support the contention that someone raised in a double bind will tend to overextend that model of interaction, and see double binds even when they are not present, resulting in an inability to interpret accurately and respond appropriately to social situations. In other words, although Charles' family life cannot be said to have caused his schizophrenia, it did increase his vulnerability to distorted perceptions of his own and other people's behavior—which, in turn, helped guarantee his future as the outsider.

What is remarkable is not the way in which my father's upbringing affected his thinking, but the fact that he was able at twenty-five to pinpoint the nature of its influence and had undertaken to offset that influence with his research in sociology. After talking with my mother and reading about the double-bind theory, I realized that my father's job at Eastern State Hospital four years earlier may have been an early attempt to understand his own interpersonal difficulties as much as it was his first attempt to be the gatekeeper. What had seemed at first to be simple irony—that he had worked at a psychiatric hospital in college only to become a patient at a psychiatric hospital decades later—may have actually been a reflection of his desire even then to take control of his emerging aberrant thought processes and his future.

After I left Williamsburg, I retraced my father's migration from the College of William and Mary to the University of North Carolina at Chapel Hill in the fall of 1965. The student population at Chapel Hill had doubled in the thirty years since his arrival, but the campus was still luxuriant, green, and full of promise. Nothing Dr. Kernodle and Dr. Rhyne had said about my father as an undergraduate prepared me for the animosity he inspired in his former professors at Chapel Hill, three of whom were still on the faculty when I visited. Ironically, their opinion had nothing to do with his alcoholism or his thinking and everything to do with his critical faculty and his aspiration of being the gatekeeper.

In the introduction to his first book, *The Language of Sociology*, my father wrote that the dissatisfaction he felt in college about sociology's lack of explanatory power developed in graduate school into "a full-blown pursuit of an answer to the question, 'Why does sociology fail to help me understand the observable behavior of men?' " In attempting to answer this question, he quickly discovered that his college professors' willingness to accept a student as an equal and to engage in no-holds-barred intellectual debate was not the norm in academia.

Dr. James Wiggins, Charles' dissertation adviser at Chapel Hill, did not need to be shown a photograph of him or be reminded when he had attended the program. He remembered his former student very well even after thirty years; he also remembered the run-ins Charles had with the faculty. "Charles was an exceptionally bright individual. Nobody ever contested that. He could handle ideas very, very well: he was always comfortable dealing with abstractions and yet seeing the connections between them and some concrete reality; he was also very skilled at being parsimonious about his thought processes. But Charles was also irreverent. He would not defer to faculty. He would continue to challenge them, including myself, about ideas that we would have and he would not hesitate to describe his disagreement in the most vehement terms."

Charles may have put aside his tough guy imitations, but he was still unwilling to capitulate when he believed he had reason on his side; a gatekeeper does not back down. The animosity he inspired among the faculty intensified with time, but never interfered with his performance. At the same time, in all fairness to the faculty, they did not allow their personal feelings to get in the way of their recognition of his accomplishments. When, for example, Charles took his written examination for the master's degree in January 1967, a semester early, the review committee noted in his records, "He is one of our problem people, very independent. Has great ability." When he passed his written examination for the Ph.D. degree ten months later, the department chairman sent him a letter of congratulations: "I was asked by the entire faculty to pass on to you their compliments for demonstrating your very considerable ability not only so adequately but also in such a relatively short period of time since you started your graduate work. It was our feeling that you show considerable promise and we thought it proper to let you know that we have high expectations of your future."

Charles' accomplishments continued apace. In the spring of 1968 he won the Bobbs-Merrill Award, given each year to an outstanding graduate student in sociology. That summer he received a National Science Foundation Excellence Grant and, at a time when it was unusual for a student to begin publishing before he received his Ph.D., his first professional article appeared in *Pacific Sociological Review*. (He would publish two more articles before completing his doctorate.) During this same period Charles wrote the book-length manuscript, *Explaining Human Behavior*, which drew on his experiences with his family, and began what would be his first published book, *The Language of Sociology*. In January 1969 he completed his doctoral dissertation and received his Ph.D. Entitled, "The Double-Bind Phenomena: A Conceptual Analysis and Empirical Proposal," his dissertation was a continuation and refinement of the research he had begun in his master's thesis.

His success at Chapel Hill notwithstanding, Charles had discovered that there was a price to be paid for being the gatekeeper. His run-ins with faculty suggested that he was going to continue to have trouble adapting to the heavily politicized world of academia as he made the transition from graduate student to sociologist. Charles had also learned that his being the outsider was less a matter of choice than he believed; he was seeing in himself disturbing patterns of thinking that ran deeper than mere bravado. It is possible, of course, that this discovery was made earlier; that the insecurity that his college professors and roommate sensed in him at William and Mary may have been an indication that he was aware of disturbing thought patterns even then. It may be that his affinity for outsiders and his interest in sociology dating all the way back to high school were attempts to understand and reign in his own behavioral aberrations, not just those of his family.

After receiving his Ph.D., Charles decided to move back to New York and look for work there. Julie, who had completed her master's degree in sociology and was eager to pursue her Ph.D. elsewhere, returned to New York with him. Looking back over thirty years at the twenty-three-year-old man she met and fell in love with at Chapel Hill, Julie was inclined to believe that his fate had been decided by then. "If I ask myself, is there anything that might have been done differently by him or circumstances that would have made the outcome different, I guess I think that the answer is no because he was so unstable and most of the controls were from without." With the benefit of hindsight, the question, perhaps, was not whether Charles would have significant trouble functioning later in life, but what form that trouble would take. His inability to entirely trust his perception of his own and other people's behavior, especially given the demands he placed on himself as the gatekeeper, left him extremely vulnerable. It is a testament to his strength of character and purpose that he managed to retain so much control over his thought processes and his life for as long as he did.

Part Two

No matter how adverse the circumstances—and mine have been adverse—there is never any reason to give up.

—Charles Lachenmeyer,
  in a letter to me, October 1986

Chapter 5

The
Father

Today the collection of Super 8 movies my father screened each year on my birthday sits in a box in the basement of the house in Pelham, alongside a dozen three-minute rolls of silent Super 8 film, home movies that were never threaded through the projector in the years my father was alive. Shot between 1971 and 1978, they highlight fishing and crabbing trips, summer excursions to the beach, and trips to Europe. I watched them for the first time, alone in the basement, the day after I returned from Burlington. It was a relief to be reminded that there had been a time when my father's world and my world were not ruled by his disorder. Since that viewing, the home movies have taken over my memories of childhood like a benevolent but persistent virus, shoring up faded recollections and overwhelming others with their immutable images.

In the earliest roll, my father and I are walking hand in hand along the shore of a lake. My mother is the director of photography. Colors are exaggerated: my hair is bright yellow; I am wearing a glowing red sweater and shiny white diapers; the grass is a brilliant green; the sky is blue enamel. I pick up an abandoned hairbrush and begin swinging it as we walk. My father takes it, wipes the dirt off, and hands it back to me. A few seconds pass before my mother begins recording again. My father and I are further along in our adventure by a few steps. I have dropped the hairbrush and replaced it with a stick. Or my father has taken the hairbrush away and given me the stick.

In the next scene my father and I are sitting on our haunches at the lake's edge. We take turns throwing pebbles into the lake.

Several years go by in a series of jump cuts and halting pans.

My father is doing jumping jacks, warming up for his morning run. I am standing next to him in a matching T-shirt and blue shorts, pumping my arms up and down and kicking my legs out in every direction, a big grin on my face. Behind us, Georgie, our overweight weimaraner, sits with his head on his paws, the picture of quiet dignity.

The next scene opens with my father and me bending over a metal bucket teeming with blue crabs, all of them keepers. The footage has a greenish tint. My father points to an enormous crab that has only one blue-tipped claw and tells me something. Sitting in the dark in the basement, my mind plays a trick on me; I hear my father's voice explaining to me that their claws grow back.

Later that day, my father and I are on a pier, fishing. The blue haze of sky and ocean behind him has transformed him into a silhouette.

A series of shaky pans across indistinct ocean vistas mark the passage of time.

The scenes become shorter. The Bronx Zoo. Animal after animal, cage after cage. The low angle of the shots and the earnest camera work suggest that I am the cameraman.

The famous blizzard of 1978. The footage is dark blue and shadowy. My father and I sled down our driveway on an old-fashioned sled we bought at a tag sale. Georgie stands at attention in a snowdrift by the garage at the bottom of the slope.

The following winter—the winter of the transient. I sneak up on my father with a snowball while he shovels the walk. My mother follows close behind with the camera, ready to document my sneak attack. My father turns, ducks. The snowball grazes the top of his head. He scoops up some snow. Snowball fight!

The trip to Greece that summer. I am wearing a Greek sailor's cap, holding my mother's hand. My father is the cameraman. Lots of shaky pans, lots of ruins. Every shot is washed out by a strong sun and out of focus, suggesting my father is drunk for most of the trip . . . ? The weakness of the images allows my memories to reassert themselves. He *was* drunk. He was losing his hold on reality. He thought the owner of the house we were renting was spying on him. He threw a glass saltshaker at my mother, which shattered on the wall between her and me, after accusing her of involvement in an unnamed conspiracy. My mother and I both started to cry. My father went home early to try to straighten himself out. Beginning of the end.

My parents drifted into marriage in January 1969 and had me, their only child, in December of that same year. They were both twenty-six years old. They moved to what I think of as my hometown, Pelham, New York, four years later. A small, conservative bedroom community only fifteen miles from Manhattan, Pelham was not as well-to-do as the towns that gave Westchester its reputation for wealth, but it was much more affluent than the neighboring city of New Rochelle and the part of the Bronx that it bordered. Despite its proximity to Manhattan, Pelham retained a small town's insularity, which I enjoyed as a young boy but grew to resent when my father's behavior propelled us into the ranks of the strange and different. The majority of husbands commuted by train to their jobs in Manhattan; the majority of wives raised children and donated time to the various community groups that helped define the town's character. Almost everyone in Pelham was white and either Protestant or Catholic. Blacks and Hispanics were relegated to New Rochelle and the Bronx, and the adjacent town of Mount Vernon. The few isolated Jewish families were default targets of adolescent pranks.

My parents were unusual by Pelham standards. They both worked full-time. They did not attend religious services. They did not socialize much with their neighbors and had no interest in community affairs. Pelham, to them, was a small front yard dominated by a large oak tree; a nice place to go for a walk; an easy commute to New York City. My parents raised me in their image; the traditions and beliefs that shaped my thinking, the good and the bad, originated in and around my home—an ungainly, wood-shingled house filled with books, situated at the top of a beautiful, suburban tree-lined street. It was there that they gave me one of the greatest gifts a parent can bestow upon a child: a firm belief in one's own potential and faith that the world will yield without protest to the honest expression of that potential.

My childhood was an endless procession of big plans, conceived, labored over, then forgotten. Whenever I was not reading, I was designing and redesigning the house I would live in when I grew up, searching the backyard for treasure, inventing board games that were going to make me rich, writing stories, or drawing in my sketchbook. I thought of myself primarily as an artist. Animals were my specialty. In retrospect, it seems as though I spent most of my free time sketching the photographs in my huge collection of animal books. My goal was to assemble enough good drawings to publish an animal book of my own.

My father not only encouraged my plans; he often collaborated with me on them. One of my *biggest* big plans was to build a museum of natural history in the garage behind our house that would rival Manhattan's American Museum of Natural History. On our daily walks with Georgie my father kept an eye out for potential finds—fallen birds' nests, unusual rocks, animal bones—and shared what he had learned during his summers exploring the woods surrounding Greenwood Lake. To supplement my already substantial nature collection, he even gave me his own childhood collection—a mounted butterfly, a prehistoric shark's tooth, and a small mountain of polished pebbles we referred to optimistically as "semiprecious stones."

My father's biggest contribution to my biggest big plan was coming up with the centerpiece for our permanent exhibit. His idea hinged upon the discovery of a dead animal. We would have traded our greatest find, an eight-inch chunk of rose quartz, for a dead squirrel or crow. Several months came and went before we got lucky. In the end, it was Georgie who found a dead crow in a bush on Harmon Avenue. It took a strong leash and my father's 220 pounds to keep him from devouring his discovery. My father walked us both home, then returned with the car, a pair of old gloves, and a garbage bag. In the basement, he transferred the crow to a large Mason jar which he filled with hydrochloric acid and buried in the backyard. He had it all worked out. The acid would eat through the feathers and flesh and leave a perfectly preserved skeleton. We would then mount the skeleton and display it in the garage, our version of the giant tyrannosaurus rex display in the American Museum of Natural History.

All those years when I planned and dreamed without worry in the safety of my parents' shadows and in the shadow of the house I loved, my parents lived in another world where the future was slowly dying. For my father there was no sudden break with reality; his was a gradual decline where a tendency toward paranoia and hostility, a misreading of people and events, slowly came to dominate his personality and his interactions with other people until, finally, the tendency and the personality were indistinguishable.

In retrospect, Charles' research on schizophrenia as a graduate student suggests a man preparing to do battle with a foe he expected to meet in the future. When he began his teaching career, however, he turned away from the subject, which raises the possibility that he no longer felt the threat of the past, of his mother, and her legacy of paranoia and manipulation. He may have believed that the danger had passed. After all, he had survived the typical age of onset for schizophrenia (late adolescence, early adulthood), and had built a life for himself far removed from his family and Brooklyn. The alternative is that he may have already been applying the lesson he would share with me sixteen years later: "No matter how adverse the circumstances, there is never any reason to give up."

The 1970s saw the beginning and end of Charles' career as an academic. When he was hired as an assistant professor of sociology at Hunter College in Manhattan in 1970, he already had an impressive list of publications to his credit: eight articles appearing in six different professional journals over the previous four years. Each article was a critical examination of different methodological issues in sociology and psychology. The following year, when he was twenty-eight, Charles' first book, *The Language of Sociology*, was published to favorable reviews. His run-ins with the faculty at Chapel Hill had apparently done nothing to temper his goal of being the gatekeeper. *The Language of Sociology* was his most ambitious effort to date. In it he took on the field of sociology as a whole, outlining a strategy for rooting the discipline more firmly as a social science with a consistent methodology. Two years later, Charles' second—and last—book, *The Essence of Social Research*, was published by the Free Press. A refinement of *The Language of Sociology*, it offered a detailed analysis of the appropriate parameters for research in the social sciences.

Although Charles was from the start a very good and committed teacher, he was unable to adapt to the subtleties of departmental politics. He made enemies as quickly teaching at Hunter as he had as a graduate student at Chapel Hill. Not even his prolific output as a writer was enough to protect him. In early 1975 he was turned down for tenure and his contract was dropped. He was stunned by the decision. For the first time he had been punished for his relentless pursuit of the role of gatekeeper and for his attendant lack of social skills. Although he began to interview immediately for another teaching position, he started drinking more and continued to brood over what had happened.

That summer, Dottie died of a heart attack at the age of seventy. At the funeral I saw my father cry for the first time. The next morning he took the train into New York City to keep an appointment for an important job interview, but did not return on the evening train. Three days later, he showed up and explained to my mother that on his way to the interview he had stopped at the Port Authority Bus Terminal and spontaneously bought a bus ticket to Dexter, Maine. After discovering that the Wassakeag School had closed down years before, he rented a room at a motel outside of town, bought a case of beer, and drank the hours away, thinking about his past. Although my father refused to say any more about his disappearance, my mother had the impression that he was attempting to sort through what role Dottie's legacy played in his current professional difficulties. Over the months that followed it became clear to my mother that her death had had a profound and enduring effect on my father. "As strange as his relationship was with his mother, while she was alive he worked very hard to keep himself in check, to hold himself together. After she died, it was as if the walls of his life had fallen away, leaving him completely exposed to the storm that was building up around him and in him."

My father was hired in the fall of 1975 as an associate professor of sociology and anthropology at St. John's University in Queens, New York. When I returned from Chapel Hill in the fall of 1996, I visited St. John's and talked with his former colleague, Dr. Theodore Kemper, who had recommended him for the position after hearing a talk he gave on *The Language of Sociology*. Dr. Kemper, a soft-spoken sociologist with a full head of white hair and a trim white beard, explained that my father was hired to set up an applied research program in sociology within the department, which he named "The Program for the Analysis, Evaluation, and Design of Planned Human Action." In addition to running the program and teaching, his responsibilities included recruiting new graduate students and securing government grants and private contracts to fund the program. It was in the process of applying for grants that my father came into contact with the large corporations and governmental agencies he would later accuse of involvement in the conspiracy.

According to Dr. Kemper, even after his negative experiences at Hunter, Charles remained recklessly outspoken in expressing his opinions on departmental issues. By the start of his second year at St. John's, he began to alienate other members of the faculty. In summing up his difficulties within the department, Dr. Kemper made use of a telling analogy. "Charles was not socially adept. Being part of a faculty is a little like being part of a family. There is the closeness of the family, but at the same time you cannot really take advantage of the affection of the family, and rely upon the fact that people love you anyway. Therefore, you have to be careful." His vulnerability was increased because his program was slow to receive outside funding and because his research reports and grant proposals had reduced his output of professional articles.

Charles was not rehired by St. John's for the 1977 academic year and the Program for the Analysis, Evaluation, and Design of Planned Human Action was discontinued. The likelihood that he might one day become one of the leading lights in sociology was rapidly diminishing. Charles was now, in the eyes of any prospective employer, "a problem case." He was hired as a Visiting Associate Professor of Management and Organizational Behavior by Rutgers University in 1977 and 1978; and as an Associate Professor of Management and General Business by Hofstra University in 1979 and 1980. Each short-term appointment that did not develop into a permanent position not only hurt his chances of securing a permanent position in the future, but made it harder for him to secure subsequent short-term appointments. Charles, who had worked so hard to define a career for himself in sociology, discovered that ability and accomplishment were not enough to sustain a productive career;

he had not learned the social skills necessary to protect himself once he had gotten where he wanted to be.

Faced with an uncertain future in academia, Charles took a calculated gamble, staking his entire career on his greatest strength—the clarity and originality of his thinking. In early 1979, in response to his academic difficulties, he revived the St. John's program as an independent business which he ran out of the basement of the house in Pelham, changing the name to the Institute for the Analysis, Evaluation, and Design of Human Action. Charles *was* the Institute. His plan was to market his skills as a gatekeeper—an analyst of social behavior and organizations—to government agencies and private companies. Toward this end, he began to self-publish a series of monographs under the aegis of the Institute, showcasing his analytic abilities in the area of applied sociology. He hoped that the Institute would, in the short term, minimize his dependence on academia and its attendant politics, and, eventually, allow him to leave it behind after the Institute developed a stable client base.

My father once described in a letter to me the theoretical underpinning of the Institute. "I tried to develop an analytic system that would prove that there is an inherent logic in situations, that, while not formal logic, still can be expressed in a similar way, and, that, while not cognitive psychology, still is deterministic of individual, and, perhaps, more importantly, of collective action, as well. I did and do maintain that this situational logic represents the true study of society in all its aspects." When I reread this after my father's death I realized that his analytic system, like his work on the double bind in graduate school a decade earlier, may have been a much more personal endeavor than its formal presentation conveyed. The former was an attempt to understand what impact his upbringing had had on his life and on his current behavior. The latter, which on the surface seemed to be an entirely impersonal extension and refinement of his work as the gatekeeper, may have been, in part, an attempt to discover the rules that time and time again had evaded my father as he struggled to become, as his colleague expressed it, "socially adept."

My father enlisted my aid in a modest way in his efforts to develop his analytic system. His first monograph, *The Limits of Planning: An Analysis*, described in a systematic way the limited efficacy of planning in organizations. To encourage me in my aspirations as an artist—and to suggest a practical way of linking my interests to a possible future career—he hired me to draw a logo for the Institute. He offered me fifty cents in royalties for every copy of the monograph sold—a significant sum of money for a ten-year-old. What I drew was a circle crisscrossed haphazardly and sloppily with straight lines. I remember feeling guilty at the time because I had not put much effort into the design, but my magical childhood was on the wane; I could sense the recent changes in my father and had lost some of my faith in him and our projects. I could tell that he was disappointed when I unveiled it, but he honored our agreement and featured the logo prominently on the back cover of the monograph with a reproduction of my signature beneath it. He continued to send me royalty checks even after the divorce, when he was struggling desperately to reestablish himself.

To this day, two boxes filled with water-damaged copies of *The Limits of Planning: An Analysis* share space in the basement of the house in Pelham with boxes of my father's other self-published monographs—*Productive Performance: An Analysis, Organizational Politicking*, and *Democracy As a Planning System*. The logo I had designed turned out to be a perfect pictorial representation of my father's future. If anyone had asked my father while at William and Mary to draw a graph representing his future, he would have drawn a long, steep ascending line from one side of the page to the other. The reality was much closer to this drawing: a small circle with straight lines firing back and forth within it like a bullet ricocheting in an enclosed space, forever trapped within the confines of his emerging disorder.

During the winter of 1979, my paternal grandfather, Bill, died of a heart attack at the age of seventy-four. His death, Dottie's death, and the years of disappointment, stress, and alcohol took their toll on my father. At the exact moment when he most needed to be able to rely on the consistency and efficacy of his thought processes, his mind began to play tricks on him. In early 1980, he sent copies of his newest monograph, *Organizational Politicking*, to his mentors, Dr. Kernodle and Dr. Rhyne, with whom he had stayed in touch since returning to visit William and Mary in 1973. After reading it, their initial enthusiasm gave way quickly to confusion. When I met Dr. Rhyne in Williamsburg, he recalled, "I was very excited about his first attempt to set up an independent institute. Then I began to scratch my head as to whether what he was doing was so far advanced that I could not follow it anymore—which was a real possibility because I had come to the conclusion that in terms of fundamental ability Charles had outgrown his professors—or whether he had taken the wrong turn somewhere. The last work raised some serious questions in my mind that said, I am not sure that Charles is, to use the old, old phrase, 'all here' anymore."

Through the systematic application of his intellect and his education, my father had successfully staved off the delusional life support system of his mother long enough to begin his own life. That life, however, was founded on the assumption that he could trust the clarity of his mind. Starting in 1980, his aberrant thought processes began, under the strain of his disappointments, to coalesce into a complex, idiosyncratic delusional system. He became convinced that what had happened to his career, dating back to his being let go from Hunter College in 1975, had been the result, not of his poor social skills, but of a coordinated conspiracy aimed at stealing from him his independent research in sociology.

The greater irony by far was that after spending so many years studying paranoid schizophrenia and investigating the possible causal relationship between his upbringing and the disorder, my father was unable to see the transformation in his thinking for what it was—the emergence of paranoid schizophrenia. This lack of insight was not the result of willful self-delusion or a sudden lack of perspicuity; it was a feature of the disorder itself. As many as 40 percent of people who suffer from schizophrenia are, as a function of their disorder, unable to examine their behavior and thought processes independently of their delusional system and constellation of symptoms; they simply do not believe that they are suffering from a mental illness.

In a letter my father wrote to me in 1989, in which he attempted to prove to me that he was *not* mentally ill, he described what had happened from his perspective. "In 1979 I self-published *Organizational Politicking* which received a big play. In that work I laid claim to an analytic system for capturing situational logic that was worth millions of dollars. But I made the mistake of saying that I was the system and the Institute nothing but a spin-off. If I had not done that, maybe they would have bought the Institute and left me alone. Instead, I became a target. Soon after I published it, I noticed that I was being followed in New York City. The people who followed me were either Air Force or CDC men. I also had reason to believe that our phone was tapped. It is my belief that the Air Force approached your mother at that time and told her of my various wanderings."

As 1980 began, my father's heavy drinking masked the origin of his increasingly strange behavior. My mother found herself married to an alcoholic who was unpredictable, unfaithful, irrational, and threatening. She warned him that she would divorce him if he did not stop drinking, and was able to convince him in May of 1980 to undergo a ten-day intensive alcoholism treatment plan at the Hazelden Foundation in Center City, Minnesota. When my father returned, his delusional thought processes were more in evidence than ever before. For the first time he openly accused my mother of collaborating with various government agencies in an attempt to exploit his analytical system. At a loss for what to do, my mother insisted that they take separate vacations that summer.

My father rented a house in Martha's Vineyard and began running a series of ads in the *Vineyard Gazette* and *The Wall Street Journal*, seeking investors for the Institute: "Publications with no competitors; demonstrated broad market; international reputation; one bidder with unsatisfactory terms. Need partner to take equity position, provide financial and expert marketing support." In his 1989 letter to me, my father explained what he believed happened next. "The Vineyard is a haven for intelligence specialists and it was my ad, I believe, that brought me to their attention. In December of 1980 I returned to Pelham. Something was immediately wrong. I thought the phone was tapped so I said some things about your mother and other people in Pelham I should not have, feeling trapped with your mother's complicity. I can still remember sitting there with the telephone receiver in hand broadcasting away. Shortly after, your mother moved out, taking you with her. Then all hell broke loose. I was led to believe that I was playing an inference-building game for your mother and remuneration for the system, so day in day out I would sit by the telephone having received cues on the street (truck signs, clipped phrases of passersby and the like) and systematically build a protocol on the basis of inferences drawn. It was a game and I would win it each day only to face the next day's task. The idea was to develop the protocol, first documenting how I did what I did (the analytic system), and then at some point after winning I would receive a contract, the protocol, and get your mother back, and I could start over with my own business."

In the months leading up to my parents' separation, my father did his best to keep the existence of the conspiracy from me. He hoped that he could convince his persecutors to withdraw, and my mother to rescind her involvement, without my ever knowing what had taken place. He did not want my excitement and optimism to be curtailed by the nightmare his world had become. So he attempted the impossible: he tried to be the father I had always known, and at the same time navigate his way through a conspiracy that was threatening to destroy him and everything he held dear.

Although I did not know what my father was thinking during those months, I could sense that something had changed in him. He looked different. He started grinding his teeth when he spoke and seemed permanently distracted. The effort to juggle two worldviews simultaneously was wearing on him. He was drinking more and was less careful to hide his drinking from me. Besieged by his delusional fears, the strain eventually became too much.

One evening, about a week after my eleventh birthday, my father and I were alone at home watching an old movie on TV. My father was sitting in the white vinyl chair in the living room, and I was sitting on the floor at his feet. He had been drinking; I could smell the beer on his breath. When the movie ended, he asked me if I wanted to go for a drive. He told me there was something he wanted to show me. I was apprehensive, sensing that something was wrong, but agreed to go with him. We drove to the other end of Pelham, near the track where he and I until recently had run every weekend with Georgie. He pulled to a stop in front of a house I had never seen before. He told me that if my mother did not stop what she was doing, he would have to divorce her; and that this was where he and I would live after the divorce. When I asked him what she had been doing, he told me all about the conspiracy and her involvement. I still remember what he said. "There are men and women of great evil in this world who will enslave you with a smile. Your mother is one of those people. That does not diminish my love of her, however. I pray that you can see this tyranny for what it is, or at least preserve the right to ask questions about it."

My father was inviting me to enter his world, to join him in a war that he could not win against an enemy that did not exist. In imposing his delusional system on me, he was, without realizing it, committing the same sin as his mother: attempting to distort his son's vision of the world to match his own. At the age of eleven I had to choose between him and my mother—a familiar enough experience for children whose parents are going through a divorce. But in this case, the two choices entailed radically different versions of reality. The first: my mother was who she had always been— warm, kind, and honest; my father was crazy and getting crazier. The second: my mother was a willing conspirator in a plot aimed at destroying my father's life; my father was a maligned genius. Even as a kid, I knew, of course, which version was real. I started to cry and asked him to take me home, which he did. I could see the hurt expression on his face as he drove me back— the sudden realization that his son was scared of him.

My mother sensed my fear in the weeks that followed. When she realized that she could no longer guarantee my emotional well-being, she told my father that she wanted a divorce. I can see my father with absolute clarity. He is standing at the foot of the stairs leading to the second floor. My mother has just told him that she is moving out of the house and is taking me with her. He sits down slowly on the bottom step and covers his face with his hands. I want to run upstairs to my room, but I cannot get by him, so I just stand there. I am crying. My mother is crying. My father is crying. Each of us knows it is over; our family has died. My mother saw freedom ahead. I did not know what to see. I think my father may have seen his future in that moment—witnessed the next fourteen years of his life, experienced in one instant the years of torment and persecution, both real and imagined, that awaited him.

In June 1981, my parents were divorced. The judge awarded my mother the house in Pelham and gave her custody of me. He also granted her a restraining order which required that my father stay away from her, from me, and from the house. Two months shy of his thirty-eighth birthday my father had lost everything that had given him stability, everything that had defined him as something other than the outsider. He moved back to Bay Ridge, Brooklyn, taking Georgie—with my mother's consent, but against my protests—and found part-time work as a taxi driver. Later that summer, the improbable happened. One of my father's former graduate students from St. John's University told Dr. Kemper that he had hailed a taxi in the city only to discover that his former professor was driving the cab. When he tried to engage my father in conversation, my father said that he could not talk freely because the cab had been bugged by the FBI.

My father and I never built a museum of natural history in the garage behind our house. It was around that time that he began to change; the jar was forgotten, the project abandoned. I can no longer remember where the jar is buried, but the first time I returned to Pelham after my father's death, I walked out into the backyard and surveyed the terrain, half-expecting to see the rusty lid poking up through the earth. I found myself wondering if my father's idea had worked. The longer I stood there the more irrational my thoughts became. I was convinced that the acid had been weak; that there was still a recognizable form imprisoned in glass somewhere beneath my feet—macerated flesh, feathers, and bone. For a moment, I believed that this form existing outside of time for so long somehow explained why things turned out the way they did for my father and me.

Chapter 6

The
Prisoner

The house in Pelham has slowly given up its secrets in the years since my father's death. Suitcases filled with old photographs and letters, empty beer cans, home movies, journals, monographs, and books have all added to my understanding of my father. But my greatest find, which I discovered after returning from Chapel Hill in the fall of 1996, was a stack of old answering machine tapes, waiting to be recycled at the bottom of a utility closet. I dug up my childhood cassette recorder, sat in my old room, and played the tapes one after the other. The answering machine was always left on in the house twenty-four hours a day following my parents' divorce, specifically to avoid my father's frequent calls, so I knew that there was a good chance that they had captured his voice.

The tapes provided a detailed reminder of what life was like in those years. As the messages faded in and out, interspersed with answering machine sound effects, I was surprised to discover evidence that daily life had continued unabated. I heard the voices of long-forgotten childhood friends asking me if I wanted to come over and play Dungeons & Dragons or Monopoly. A neighbor called to ask if I would look after their cat while they were away. My pediatrician left a message for my mother that the tests had come back positive; I did have strep throat. I even heard my own childhood voice asking my mother if I could stay overnight at my best friend Frankie's house.

When I finally heard my father's voice, it sounded exactly the way it did in my memory. The last two tapes, dating from 1982, contained message after message from him. He was convinced by then that everything he said into the answering machine was being transcribed and disseminated by the FBI and CIA. Some messages were the slurred, profane ramblings of a frightened, drunk man. Others were carefully prepared statements about the current status of the persecution of which he understood himself to be the victim. In one message, my father revealed that in March 1981, three months after my parents' separation, he had tried to kill himself.

"It's me. As promised, here is the letter. William Casey, Director, CIA. Sir, on or about March 1981 your agency in cooperation with AT&T, the Pelham police department, and numerous other agencies did try to have me commit suicide in the following manner. My then wife deserted me at your instigation, taking my son with her. I was forced into isolation by conspiratorial design. The instant coffee in the house had been adulterated with a depressant. I was constantly harassed on the telephone, in my car, on foot by automobiles, and I still am. Although unaware of it at the time, I had had this mind-reading technology applied to me, which made my every physical condition knowable to you. As a result of this I did actively seek ways to kill myself. One evening I recall searching the bathroom cabinets for razor blades and drugs. At every stage of this process those responsible were aware of my dire mental state and my active search for available means. Have a good day."

As many as 10 percent of people suffering from schizophrenia commit suicide to escape the horrors of the disorder. Listening to his message again, as an adult, I could hear the fear in his voice. As a child, coming home from school and playing his messages secretly while my mother was still at work, the only fear I felt was my own. I was scared that he might hurt my mother. I was also scared that his paranoia might expand to include me; that he might one day become capable of hurting me. Fifteen years later, his voice continued to make me afraid, but it was a different kind of fear. I felt the way I felt when I saw the transient for the first time; I knew that I was witnessing something terrible, something that was not supposed to be. But it was more than that. Hearing his voice again was like standing in a hospital elevator next to someone lying unconscious on a stretcher; it was the fear of standing too close to death, in this case, the death of a mind.

After a short high-pitched beep, my father's voice faded up again in the middle of a sentence, his bravado almost masking the undercurrent of fear. Having resisted the encouragement to commit suicide, he was determined to fight back by exposing the conspiracy to the world. Here again was the outsider insisting that he be treated fairly, the gatekeeper dedicated to imposing reason on an irrational world. "—I swear to God almighty that I am not joking, that it has gone way too far, that I have been humiliated and disgraced too much, that you have kidnapped my son—and it *is* kidnapping—and I am trying to behave in the most appropriate fashion in protecting my rights. No matter what attempts are made at amends or what you people would call amends, absolutely everything that has occurred here, everything that you have promulgated and promoted and helped do, will in fact be published; and I assure you that what it looks like is not very nice. And I will be doing that directly for my son, so that you people cannot fool with pictorial representations and rewriting history. It might take me ten years to do it, but I assure you that that is exactly what is going to happen. I swear to good God almighty that I will not stop as long as I live until there is judicial determination and procedural retribution for what you have done, the big companies, AT&T, the CIA, the government and everybody else. If it takes me ten years, this will not be part of any game."

The loss of his wife, his son, and his house so soon after the derailment of his academic career and death of his parents fueled the growth of Charles' delusional system and inspired him to take great personal risks. Although Charles no longer had a steady income, starting in 1982 he began to liquidate the modest stock portfolio he had received in the divorce settlement in order to make good on his promise to publish the details of the conspiracy against him. He stopped writing monographs utilizing his analytic system and began to publish a monthly series of delusional newsletters under the rubric of the Institute. Charles published fifteen issues overall with titles like *How to Destroy Freedom and the World (An Open Letter to the KGB and the CIA)*, *Responsibility, or a Love Letter to My Son, the Hostage, from His Father, the Political Prisoner*, and *Democracy and Free Enterprise as Negative Utopia*, and sent them to family members, friends, and public figures all over the world, hoping to rally support to his cause and embarrass his persecutors into capitulating. Surprisingly, he also received a significant number of subscription orders from people throughout the country whose own conspiracy theories, whether inspired by mental illness or not, dovetailed with his delusions.

Charles brought all of his intelligence and years of training as a sociologist to bear in writing the newsletters. They are brilliant in their complexity and heartwrenching in their articulation of the suffering someone with paranoid schizophrenia endures. Nowhere in them, however, is the word "schizophrenia" used; he was still completely unaware that he was ill. His delusional system recast his experience of the symptoms of paranoid schizophrenia as an elaborate social experiment imposed on him by his persecutors. He believed that his persecutors had stripped him of everything he held dear in an attempt to force him to develop a protocol for his analytic system. When that failed, they devised a way of extracting that system from his head—making him the first subject of a new kind of social experiment, which he dubbed "Thought Control." Beginning with his first newsletter, *Thought Control and Technological Slavery in America (?)*, he set out to describe Thought Control and to reveal the experiment's inherent immorality to the world.

Thought Control had two components. Charles became aware of the first component—the omnipotence of his persecutors—just prior to the separation. He realized that they had co-opted almost everyone imaginable in their effort to observe, control, and manipulate his actions. "If I appended a list of participants to this newsletter, it would include past employers and associates, friends and family, banks, insurance companies, major newspapers, TV stations, radio stations, public utilities, religious and women's groups, veterans' organizations, private corporations, as well as every governmental agency imaginable from the Office of the President of the United States to the IRS to US Customs to the Parking Violations Bureau of New York City. The key question is 'who has not participated?' not 'who has participated?' " The pervasiveness of conspiratorial participation meant that his persecutors were

The Outsider

The Gatekeeper

The Sociologist

The Father

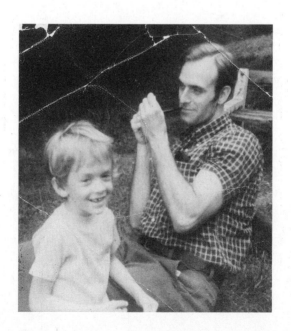

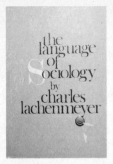

The Father

The Prisoner

N.H. STATE HOSPITAL, CONCORD, N.H.

The Prisoner

The Schizophrenic

The Stranger

AT THE BROOKLYN END OF THE BRIDGE.
Slightly confusing to a Stranger.

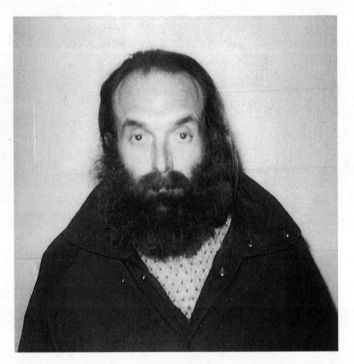

The Thief

able to exercise total control over his social environment. He lived every waking hour of every day in purposefully structured social situations; there was no such thing as chance in the new world in which he found himself.

Three months after the divorce, Charles discovered the second component of Thought Control. "Since August of 1981 my conscious thoughts have been read at a distance. All of my possible defensive or evasive tactics are known as I think about them. I cannot escape." To account for his persecutors' apparent ability to read his thoughts, Charles postulated the development of a new technology: "I believe that I ingested a low grade radioactive substance that was purposefully implanted in my food. There is no external apparatus or any toxic reactions in the blood or any other physical manifestations. Recording of thoughts is accomplished either via heat sensors or the technology in radio telescopes. Great distances are involved. Satellites may even be being used. In effect, I have been converted into a walking radio transmitter with no on/off switch."

At the end of the first newsletter, Charles explained how these components combined to make up Thought Control. "Conscious thoughts are read at a distance and environmental cues are altered so as to effect changes in these thoughts. Whereas in brainwashing, what a person is thinking is inferred by the interrogator, with Thought Control the actual inferences of the subject are read and manipulated. Direct intervention in mental processes is therefore possible." Thought Control enabled Charles' persecutors to plug into his thoughts twenty-four hours a day, allowing them to alter his social world at will and thereby modify, curtail, or encourage his thought processes at any given moment.

"An elaborate system of signs and gestures has been worked out in an attempt to control what I observe and what I perceive and how I interpret it: e.g., signs have been worked out that once decoded read as suggestions that I take a particular type of action with respect to a particular private issue. But the experiment has not stopped there. The contents of my personal, private conversations have been broadcast widely. Past mistakes and accomplishments have been ridiculed and demeaned. The content of my dreams has even been externalized, acted out, and mocked by members of the public, coached so to do. Worse, my most hostile or scurrilous thoughts are reported to and responded to by complete strangers. I am what my most negative and fleeting thoughts would make me. And I am consistently punished for those thoughts by the same agents that give rise to them. There is only one word to describe the world in which I am living: hell."

By the time he wrote the second newsletter, Charles was convinced that the goals of his persecutors had extended beyond the mere desire to steal his analytic system. "They want to fully develop the technology of Thought Control with me as a guinea pig. Their goal: to implement an extensive and far-reaching program of personality change." The means had become the end, which meant that there was now no way to predict if or when the experiment would be voluntarily terminated. Aware that the most effective way of converting people to his cause was to make them understand that what had happened to him could have an impact on them and their lives, he warned prospective readers of his newsletters not to dismiss him as a special case; if his thoughts and behaviors could be systematically altered against his will, the same could and probably would eventually happen to them.

My father sent me each of his delusional newsletters as he wrote them, starting in early 1982, when I was twelve years old. They were roughly the size and shape of a business envelope, thirty to forty pages long, stapled, with a beige card stock cover. Each one smelled of his cigars. I pored over them, reading and rereading them with a dictionary in hand. I knew by that point that my father's deterioration was the result, not simply of alcoholism, but of mental illness. Under the influence of his newsletters, correspondence, and answering machine messages, I became obsessed with understanding what was happening to him. I needed to understand how *my* father—fellow adventurer, collaborator on all my big plans, the man whom I most wanted to be like when I grew up—had been transformed into the person I was most afraid of in the world. Answering that question was the last big plan of my childhood.

After reading all of my father's old books on mental

illness—he had left most of them behind when he moved out—I slowly came to the conclusion that his symptoms most closely matched those of paranoid schizophrenia. I learned from my reading that there was a genetic component to the disorder; if a parent has schizophrenia, their children's chances of developing schizophrenia are ten times greater than that of the rest of the population. This discovery undermined the pride I felt when I recognized qualities in myself that reminded me of who my father used to be, by instilling in me the fear that if I were too much like him, I might share his fate. I was able to keep that fear more or less in check, however, by telling myself that worrying about such a possibility would, if anything, increase the likelihood of it coming to pass.

My fears and my sense of loss combined with the rush of hormones to transform me into a self-conscious, introverted adolescent who obsessed about his father and his disorder even as I tried to keep to a minimum the amount of contact between us. I seldom responded to the steady influx of letters and newsletters and never picked up the phone when it rang—but I always ran to the machine and turned up the volume, just in case it was him.

I did not know then that my father had done his graduate work on schizophrenia. Schizophrenia did not in his case—and does not as a rule—destroy a person's memory. My father was aware that the fact that he had once been concerned about developing schizophrenia and was now, from an external perspective, exhibiting symptoms of the disorder, could affect the credibility of his claims regarding Thought Control. In the second newsletter in the series, *Thought Control and Technological Slavery in America (?)*, Issue 2, he attacked the problem directly. "If I protest too much or too effectively or am deemed to be unnecessarily vindictive in my protests, depending on the opinion of my persecutors, I face the prospect of having this experiment terminated, followed by mass denial of the truth. Thus, I face the ultimate threat of being labeled as psychiatrically ill by them."

My father believed that his persecutors had specifically designed the experiment in such a way that his protests would resemble the symptoms of schizophrenia. Using their new technology to access his memories, they had found his Achilles' heel—his past private fears about his mental health—and were exploiting that old fear in their effort to control him. His response reflected both his determination and the resiliency of his delusional perspective. "There is only one thing wrong with this strategy: the truth is not determined by consensus any more than are the laws of Nature determined by man."

Over the course of 1982, Charles' condition continued to deteriorate. His newsletters documented that deterioration, albeit as an expression of the evolution of the Thought Control experiment. In May 1982 his persecutors made a major improvement to their thought-reading technology. Up until then, they had only been able to read his thoughts; now they were able to transmit messages to him in the form of voices that he alone heard. Charles came up with a new strategy for coping with what he referred to as his "technological transformation." "I would respond with reasoned argument in the form of 'broadcasts,' some, I am embarrassed to say, in public. But I was defining a whole different level of reality." In other words, in May of 1982 Charles began talking aloud to himself—one of the hallmarks of schizophrenia.

In early 1983, Charles decided that he had had enough. After threatening repeatedly in his newsletters to leave the country if his persecutors did not end their experiment, he crossed the border into Canada and rented an apartment in Quebec. He had assumed that the experiment was national in scope and was surprised and frightened when the harassment continued unchecked. After getting in a serious car accident a few weeks after arriving—which he believed was a crude attempt to silence him—he moved back to New York State. Charles kept on the move, living for a couple of months at a time in different towns upstate. His behavior was by then strange enough that he quickly alienated the locals wherever he was living. A series of police reports across the state document him screaming out loud late at night in his apartment, going through his neighbors' mail, and talking to himself in restaurants. When he became too conspicuous, he moved on, always to a town or city with access to a university and university library. The pattern would then repeat itself.

Charles' great fear was no longer that his persecutors would end the experiment without explanation or redress, leaving him to explain what on the surface seemed to be very disturbed behavior. His experiences in Canada had confirmed for him that the experiment was not going to end any time soon. What he feared most was escalation. In one of his last newsletters, self-published in the spring of 1983, Charles summed up his persecutors' accomplishments to date and predicted his own future. "Through fraudulent legal proceedings in a systematic stepwise process everything that I possessed was taken away from me: my business, my house, my wife, my son, my car, etc. The list of 'take aways' extended to social approval, and to my very identity and peace of mind. Ultimately, I am to be denied my freedom through psychiatric entrapment. The biggest 'take away' will be the truth as to my altered state after my mind has been 'jacked up' into a rage against the fates. Thus, Thought Control followed by complaint will be followed by prison or psychiatric confinement." In other words, Charles was afraid that his persecutors, in order to have more control over his freedom of movement and action, would at some point try to trap him into committing an illegal act that would land him in a psychiatric hospital.

Charles responded to this threat in the fall of 1983 by leaving New York State behind for good and renting a house in sparsely populated Eastman, a small, wooded residential community near the town of Grantham, New Hampshire. He also stopped self-publishing his newsletters and abandoned the Institute. He hoped that if he withdrew and lay low for a while, he might be able to avoid an escalation in his persecutors' punitive efforts, and force them through attrition to abandon their experiment, or find a new experimental subject. He also realized that if his mind were jacked up into a rage against the fates, he was less likely to lose control and hurt someone or break the law living alone in the woods.

My father emerged from hiding in December 1983, showing up unexpectedly in Pelham for my fourteenth birthday. I was playing kickball in the street with a handful of friends when he pulled up in the beige station wagon he had inherited from his father. Fear that my father would embarrass me in front of my friends preempted any happiness I might have felt, knowing not only that he had remembered my birthday, but that he had driven more than two hundred miles to see me. After hugging me so hard that my back cracked, he held me at arm's length, smiled, and told me how wide my shoulders were becoming. When my mother came out of the house, he asked her if we could take a short walk around the block. Because he seemed to be both sober and stable, she reluctantly consented.

My father was starved for news about me and what I had been up to over the previous two and one-half years. In the time it took us to walk down the hill, turn right onto Harmon Avenue—walking past the spot where years before we had found the crow with Georgie—make a second right onto Storer Avenue, a third right onto Washington Avenue, and turn back onto my block, he asked me so many questions that I almost ran out of breath answering him. How did I like school? How was my drawing progressing? Did I have a girlfriend? What were my friends like? Did I ever go fishing anymore? Had I added anything to my nature collection? Had I gotten all of his letters?

Trying his best to reintroduce some normalcy into our relationship in those few minutes, my father made no mention of the conspiracy or Thought Control or the divorce. I answered all of his questions, but was unable to shake my apprehension; whenever he spoke, I heard echoes of his answering machine messages and newsletters. I did not get up the nerve to ask about them or about my guess as to his diagnosis. Just before the house came into view at the top of the hill, he opened his wallet and gave me a twenty dollar bill, explaining that he had not had time to buy me a real present. I took the twenty and thanked him. Back in front of the house, he hugged me, let me go, and then started to hug me again. I squirmed out of his arms and ran to rejoin my friends. I was too young to worry that I might never see him again, or that our second, broken hug might be our last.

I drove to Eastman during the winter of 1996, in a blizzard that deposited half a foot of snow over most of New Hampshire. Using my father's police and court records, I had located several people who knew him when he lived there. Given his condition at the time, I was surprised to learn that he had made a new friend in Eastman. When my father dropped off his rent check at the beginning of each month, the elderly realtor who had rented him his house always asked him to sit and visit with her over a cup of coffee. On the strength of her memory of those conversations, she not only agreed to meet with me to talk about my father; she baked an apple pie in honor of the occasion.

The realtor recalled that my father talked a lot about me during their visits, sharing his memories of our past and expressing frustration that his efforts to reach me by telephone were never successful. The subject he returned to most often, however, was Dottie. "I was old enough to be his mother and he knew that I had sons and daughters his age. He was always asking me, 'If you were my mother, what would you have done if I did so-and-so?' Then he would say something a child was apt to do. I got the feeling that he was trying to figure out what was causing his problems, so I tried to be what help I could." Sitting with his friend, discussing her approach to parenting, my father seemed to still be grappling with the effects his mother had had on his life, fifteen years after completing his dissertation on the double-bind theory. The questions he asked her raise the possibility that his persecutors' attempts to get him to doubt his sanity were not entirely without results during this volatile period in his life.

Before leaving, I asked the realtor what she knew about what happened to my father in Eastman. She told me that there seemed to have been some misunderstandings between him and some of their neighbors, but that she never fully understood why my father left Eastman so abruptly in June 1984. I thanked her for her kindness, then trudged through the snow to find the two neighbors who had filed police reports against my father twelve years before.

Six months after his visit to Pelham, Charles' prediction about his future came to pass: jacked up into a rage against the fates by his suffering and his confusion, for the first and only time his aberrant behavior crossed the line into violence. His police records from New Hampshire document what happened. One evening in early June, Charles took Georgie for his evening walk. When they were almost home Georgie chased a squirrel into the woods and disappeared. Early the next morning, when Georgie still had not returned, Charles became convinced that his persecutors had taken his only companion from him to punish him further. He began pounding on his next-door neighbor's kitchen window while she was preparing breakfast, shouting through the glass that he knew that she had stolen his dog. The window shattered under the impact and he stormed off.

Later that day, while Charles was driving down Eastman Road looking for Georgie, a car cut in front of him. Charles followed the driver into her driveway, shouted at her to leave him alone, then punched her in the face. He was certain that she had cut in front of him to send him a pointed warning about the destructive direction in which his thoughts were heading. The police found Charles later that evening at home—Georgie had wandered back hours before—and arrested him. He spent the night in jail. The next morning the police transferred him to New Hampshire Hospital in Concord for a psychiatric evaluation, and dropped Georgie off at a local veterinary clinic to await word on his owner's fate.

I am ashamed to admit that because of the prevalence of stories in the media about people with schizophrenia committing violent crimes, one of my great fears as I began to investigate my father's life was that I would uncover evidence that he had killed someone. The truth is, however, that despite the media's generally sensational and distorted portrayal of people with schizophrenia, most are not violent. If anything, they tend to withdraw and stay to themselves, as my father tried to do for much of his life after onset. The extensive media coverage of the relatively few violent crimes committed by people with schizophrenia and the concomitant lack of coverage of their struggles and accomplishments are not an accurate reflection of the disorder; it is a telling indication of the media and the public's indifference to the plight of people with schizophrenia in this country—unless and until they feel directly threatened by the desperate, irrational acts the disorder leads a few of their number to commit.

When I arrived at New Hampshire Hospital it was still snowing hard. In the mid-1950s, there were approximately 2,000 patients there. When my father was committed thirty years later, there were only 250 patients. Today there are 120. The Peasely Building, where they put my father, was shut down in 1986 in response to the declining number of patients. The front portion of the building was converted into a cluster of administrative offices. Waiting for me in one of the offices was a copy of my father's hospital records, which I had requested before arriving, and the groundskeeper, who took me on a tour of the rest of the building.

The wings on either side of the Peasely Building, where the patients used to be housed, were wasting away like the vestigial appendages of a huge mythical beast. Ten New Hampshire winters without water, heat, or electricity had achieved the level of destruction of a massive conflagration. Most of the wire-reinforced windows were cracked or broken. Ribbons of peeling paint hung from the ceiling, held in place, it seemed, by a complex network of cobwebs. The floor was invisible under a layer of paint chips and dirt. Dried carcasses of pigeons and crows that had flown in through the windows and never found their way out again lay half-buried among the ruins. The floor-to-ceiling prison gates at the entrance to each ward and the smaller gates that served as doors to each patient's tiny cell were covered with rust.

The only evidence that established that I was in a hospital, not an abandoned prison, other than a few torn, faded posters instructing patients how they should behave on the ward, were the dozens of crude paintings that decorated the walls of the main hallway in P-1, my father's ward. When I asked about them, the groundskeeper informed me that they were all painted by a single patient with schizophrenia who was at New Hampshire Hospital in the mid-1960s. The peeling paint and half-light imbued the images with a degree of depth and mystery entirely in keeping with their surroundings. The subject of each painting was different—roaring waterfalls; lions silhouetted by a sunset on the Sahara plains; a gray cat sitting by an open window, looking out at a vast, colorful garden—but the theme was always the same: freedom.

The decline in the number of patients at state hospitals began in the mid-1960s, when the paintings covering the walls of P-1 were new and my father was still a young attendant and self-styled researcher at another hospital hundreds of miles to the south. Three developments combined to set in motion a trend toward deinstitutionalization: the introduction in the 1950s of Thorazine, the first antipsychotic medication for the treatment of schizophrenia; growing national concern about the cost of inpatient care; and revelations about the deplorable conditions at many psychiatric hospitals, which resulted in increased public interest in protecting the civil liberties of the mentally ill.

In response, in 1963 the Community Mental Health Centers Act was passed to fund the development nationally of shelters, community mental health centers, and community housing—an infrastructure intended to supplant the hospital as the primary method of care for the mentally ill. At the same time, the laws regarding involuntary commitment became more stringent. Although the laws varied from state to state, they usually entailed a variation of the following: the individual in question had to pose a clearly defined danger to himself or others.

A mass exodus of patients into the community followed in the 1960s, 1970s, and 1980s. This transformation of the mental health care system ultimately failed because the infrastructure was never properly funded, and because those community mental health centers that were established frequently devolved into therapy centers for more healthy, functional people. Today, as a result of the failure of deinstitutionalization, more than 60 percent of people with mental illnesses receive inadequate care and the mentally ill make up approximately one-third of the nation's homeless.

Twenty years after first attempting to develop a new point of view toward mental illness, Charles became Patient No. 64884 at New Hampshire Hospital. For the first time, his amalgam of strange behaviors was given a formal diagnosis: chronic paranoid schizophrenia. The progress notes in his file—handwritten entries by different members of the staff that document a patient's progress, changes in symptoms, and significant statements or behaviors—attest to his conviction that his hospitalization represented an escalation in the experiment. He believed that his commitment was a calculated attempt to weaken his faith in his own sanity by isolating him from the real world and forcing him to take on the role of patient and prisoner. From the start, Charles was convinced that the staff was in on the conspiracy, and that any cooperation on his part would be interpreted by them as an admission that he might be mentally ill. Not surprisingly, he rejected every attempt to convince him to accept psychiatric medication to help alleviate his symptoms. He also refused to provide any information about his background or personal history, which helped make him an enigmatic figure on the ward.

Charles spent most of each day sitting in the same chair, silhouetted by the windows at the far end of the ward. He wrote for hours at a time on small pads of paper in a tiny script, and never showed anyone what he was working on. He kept to himself, never socializing with the other patients or the staff. The only time he stopped writing was to eat meals or to work out in the weight room, which he did obsessively. His evident hostility over his imprisonment, the violent acts that got him committed, and his imposing stature combined to make the attendants, nurses, and doctors wary of him. There was considerable concern among the staff and administration at the hospital that he would attempt to break out. As a result, he was never allowed off the ward with the other patients.

It was not until September, when Charles wrote a letter to Clifford, accusing him of involvement in the conspiracy, that the staff was able to piece together any of his personal history. Clifford contacted the hospital to find out what had happened and provided the staff with background information on Charles. They were shocked to discover that the only patient on the ward who really scared them had been a college professor. Clifford's comments, duly recorded by the staff, together with the police reports and progress notes, constituted the beginning of Charles' psychiatric records—a collection of files that would, at the time of his death, total more than a thousand pages.

Although the staff had no way of knowing it, Clifford had recounted the family history from the vantage point of Christian Science. Dottie and Bill were wonderful parents. There were no problems in the Lachenmeyer family. According to Clifford, Charles' outcome was the result of runaway arrogance and alcoholism, tendencies he had embraced after leaving home. The subtext was clear: he was spiritually weak, a nonbeliever. Dottie's delusional system, which Charles had fought so hard to escape, had come back to haunt him in his psychiatric records.

A year passed without Charles being able to set foot outside or look at the sky except through a prism of wire mesh. In June 1985, in response to his continued refusal to accept treatment, the Court of Probate of Merrimack County, New Hampshire, ruled that Charles was incapacitated by his disorder and that legal guardianship was "necessary as a means of providing continuing care, supervision, and rehabilitation." This is often necessary for patients suffering from schizophrenia, who would, under the influence of their delusional system, otherwise continue to refuse treatment indefinitely. Typically, the legal guardian meets with the patient only when legal issues arise related to treatment. The terms of Charles' guardianship were very limited. His guardian had the right to make decisions regarding his need for treatment, but did not have the right to control his finances or hinder his movements upon release from the hospital. On the recommendation of Charles' psychiatrist at New Hampshire Hospital, the guardian immediately authorized that he be involuntarily medicated with the antipsychotic medication Haloperidol.

Antipsychotic medication had a significant but limited impact on Charles' thought processes. He quickly became less hostile and guarded. He continued to voice delusional ideas, but with much decreased emphasis. Significantly, he was still unable to recognize that he was mentally ill or make a connection between his improved condition and his medication. According to his progress notes, "Although he reluctantly accepts the inevitability of the medication, he has never fully recognized its beneficial effects. He has said, for example, that he does not know why people have stopped reading his mind, but that it is because they have stopped that he has stopped talking to himself."

Although Charles' symptoms remained, it was clear that he was no longer a danger to himself or others. Preparations were begun for his conditional discharge. Charles signed a statement agreeing to meet weekly with a case manager at a mental health center in Lebanon after his release, and to continue to take his medication voluntarily; failure to comply would result in his return to the hospital. A social worker on staff at the hospital helped him locate a one-room efficiency in Lebanon, New Hampshire, a short bus ride away from Dartmouth College. Through his legal guardian he applied for and began to receive $604 a month in Supplemental Security Income (SSI), disability-related income provided by the Social Security Administration.

When Charles began to reinitiate contact with the outside world, he discovered that he had lost nearly all of his material possessions while preoccupied with fending off his persecutors in the hospital. The garage that had agreed to store his car sold it when they did not receive the monthly payments. Georgie was adopted by another family after he failed to pay the local veterinarian's kennel fees. At the time Charles was committed, he had asked the owner of the house he had rented in Eastman if he could store a few of his most important possessions in the basement, including ten years' worth of journals containing ideas for future sociological research. She had said yes. When he contacted her after his release, however, she told him that everything had been destroyed by water damage after a flood.

In October 1985, after spending sixteen consecutive months at the state hospital, Charles was released. From his perspective, his commitment had not been a coordinated attempt to improve his stability and level of social functioning; it had been the realization of his worst fear. Stripped of the few things that had continued to give his life meaning, Charles had been handed a diagnosis of paranoid schizophrenia, a prescription for Haloperidol (to be taken once a day orally), a check for $604 a month in SSI, and the threat that if he tried too hard to escape the label of schizophrenic, his conditional discharge would be revoked and he would be readmitted. He was trapped. Only as long as he actively accepted and cultivated a diagnosis of paranoid schizophrenia would he be granted a reprieve as the prisoner. If he protested his diagnosis in word or deed, his physical freedom would again be taken from him until he relented. His persecutors had made good on their ultimate threat: to not admit to what they had done and to simultaneously have him labeled mentally ill, leaving him alone in his conviction that he was sane.

Chapter 7

The
Schizophrenic

In June 1984, when I was fourteen, my father's letters suddenly stopped coming. It is a testament to my youth that I did not worry that my father had died; I worried that he had forgotten me. His next letter arrived in October 1985, the month he was released from New Hampshire Hospital. I had thought about him often during the intervening sixteen months of silence, but I was a teenager and thought about myself more. I was consumed with my efforts to survive a typically awkward and miserable adolescence. A large part of those efforts, ironically, centered on my growing interest in mental illness. I read religiously about schizophrenia and began to idolize the creative works of the mentally ill. I marveled at the fragility of the mind and at how we all take for granted the solidity and immutability of our sense of self. When my father began writing again after his release, he did not know that his son, then almost sixteen, had built his emerging sense of self around the fact that he had a father who suffered from schizophrenia.

In his correspondence with me, my father worked hard to resume a more normal, parental role in my life. He was careful not to mention his hospitalization, his diagnosis, or the conspiracy. He did his best to nurture my interests from afar and to encourage my education. Aware of my love of poetry, for example, he sent me a large poetry bibliography, which he spent a week assembling at the Dartmouth Library. He also bought me a collection of books on philosophy, including works by Wittgenstein, Berkeley, and Quine. In the letter that accompanied the books, he wrote, "What I am trying to do is fill up your library with all the books you will need to call yourself educated, at least in my opinion."

For my sixteenth birthday my father sent me a sampling of his current writing. It was all he could afford to give me; it was also the thing that meant more to him than anything else in the world. The accompanying letter made clear that he had refused to let Thought Control, his diagnosis, or the memory of his sixteen months at the state hospital discourage him or slow him down. He wrote about his renewed interest in sociology. He had revived the Institute and his investigation of situational logic. What he had earlier called his analytic system he now referred to as Analytic Space. He ended his letter with words of cautious optimism about the future:

> *A word of advice for you for your future based on a father's bitter experience: the only real investment you have is yourself and what you can do. Nobody*

*can take that away from you; and it is only in the
process of self-growth which is continual that you
realize this investment. It has not been easy for me
over the last five years, but I am very lucky to have
rediscovered this. It has kept me on a work schedule
at Dartmouth that has kept me from getting too
depressed or scared. I honestly do not know how anybody can retire—I have also discovered that for me
this will be impossible.*

*My thoughts and heart are always with you. If
you need anything, let me know.*

Love, Dad.

I was as confused by my father's apparent return to
normalcy as I had been by his initial transformation into
the schizophrenic. I scoured each of his letters for evidence of his former symptoms, and, to my surprise, found
none. Although I do not remember consciously making
this decision, it is clear to me now that I had decided that
I would stay in touch with my father only if he continued
not to exhibit any symptoms. Given that there is no cure
for schizophrenia and given the limited efficacy of current methods of treatment, this was asking too much. My
confusion and wariness kept me from responding consistently to his letters or doing much to encourage his efforts
to recover the relationship we had once had.

I discovered the effect my confusion had on my
father from his case manager in Lebanon, New

Hampshire. I interviewed John Englund, a soft-spoken man with pale skin and white hair, during the winter of 1996 in the same office in which he had counseled my father ten years before. At almost every meeting, my father expressed frustration about how infrequently I wrote. He would pace the floor when he talked about me, his voice would break, and tears would come to his eyes. He continued to write to me, however, and to try not to pressure me into writing back. Summing up my importance in his life, Englund told me, "His relationship with you was the one place in his life where he felt hope and a connection. I felt that if you and he did not maintain contact, that would be severing the last wire for him." I asked Englund to repeat what he had said, not because I had not heard him or because it had not registered, but to work those words into me, so that I could not rationalize them away later, sitting in my apartment in Manhattan, reconstructing the meeting in my head. It was not until I heard those words that I understood exactly how alone my father was during the years following the divorce, and my role in his increasing sense of isolation.

Charles' determination to reclaim his past extended to his efforts to find a teaching position. Englund recalled that "his resolve and the rationality of his approach were nothing less than heroic. I did not know how to account for it except that he was a person of great intellect and I think that overrode some of the limitations imposed on him by the disorder." Although Charles still evidenced delusions of grandeur and paranoia during their weekly meetings, his query letters to universities, which he wrote by the dozen on a secondhand type-writer, were always perfectly appropriate in tone and content. His résumé, which he reproduced from memory after his conditional discharge, faithfully recorded his academic accomplishments and publications without embellishment. He also included information about his current research into Analytic Space and his earlier monographs on situational logic, but never mentioned his delusional newsletters or broached the subject of Thought Control. Charles' credentials and manner of presentation were sufficiently impressive that he was able to garner several interviews with area universities.

In December 1985, only two months after his conditional discharge, Charles had his first breakthrough on the job front. He was hired to teach an introductory sociology course entitled "Sociological Theories and Practices" at Lebanon College, beginning in March 1986. The pay was negligible, but it was his first opportunity to begin to close the gap recent events had left in his résumé, which was critical if he were to have any hope of eventually returning to academia full-time. Over the next few months, Charles devoted a lot of time to preparing for the course. His excitement about the chance to teach again was apparent during his weekly meetings with Englund, where the course was a frequent topic of conversation. Charles explained the themes he planned to emphasize. He tried his lectures out on Englund. In a moment of rare candor, he even reminisced about his first classes in sociology at William and Mary and expressed the hope that he might inspire some of his students the way his former professors had inspired him.

Two days before classes were supposed to start, Charles received a call from Lebanon College, informing him that the course had been canceled due to low enrollment. When he met with Englund later that morning he admitted that he had had to pull himself together on the walk on the way over. Charles' disappointment led to a burgeoning of his delusional system. At their next meeting, he exhibited a dramatic increase in anxiety, hostility, and paranoia. Englund began to receive complaints about him from the community. Dartmouth College issued a trespass complaint forbidding him from returning to their library after he accused a librarian of spying on him. His neighbors wrote a joint letter to his landlady, which she forwarded to Englund, documenting a spate of bizarre behavior: he tore open their mail; he shouted threats and obscenities when he was alone in his apartment late at night; he was even observed on one occasion peeing out his window.

Charles' first attempt to escape his new identity as the schizophrenic was short-lived. On April 3, 1986, he was readmitted to New Hampshire Hospital for an emergency evaluation. At admission, Charles confessed that he had not taken his medication during the previous three months. In light of his inability to understand that he was mentally ill, his noncompliance was a practical response to the medication's side effects. Short-term side effects of Haloperidol, a major tranquilizer, include drowsiness, restlessness, dry mouth, and blurring of vision. Long-term side effects can include weight gain, a decrease in sexual drive, and an increase in sexual dysfunction, which can exert a profound effect on mood and quality of life. The more serious side effects include extrapyramidal symptoms—uncontrolled tremors and muscle stiffness—and Tardive Dyskinesia, a disorder characterized by involuntary writhing movements often affecting the mouth, lips, and tongue, and extremities. Tardive Dyskinesia occurs in about 15 to 20 percent of patients who receive the older antipsychotic medications like Haloperidol, and can lead to social withdrawal.

Charles told his treatment team that he believed that the reason he had not been able to find a full-time teaching position was because he was exhibiting extrapyramidal symptoms during job interviews. This was entirely possible. The staff at the state hospital wrote in his progress notes around this time, "He often exhibits severe jerky, twisting movements of his forearms and hands while his elbows are resting on the arm rests of his favorite chair. In an attempt to keep the tremors under control he sometimes grips the arm rests or his knees hard enough to turn his knuckles white with the effort." Although Charles never stated it explicitly, Englund had the impression that Charles saw the medication's side effects as another form of persecution—both a painful reminder that he had been labeled a paranoid schizophrenic and a calculated attempt to prevent him from finding work.

With the consent of his legal guardian, Charles was given a prescription for Cogentin, a medication which reduces extrapyramidal symptoms. He was also prescribed a monthly injection of Haloperidol to replace his daily pills, in order to make his compliance easier to monitor after discharge. His condition quickly improved and preparations were begun for his release. Although compliance with medication reduces the intensity and frequency of relapses, it does not prevent them. Reflecting this, the staff at New Hampshire Hospital did not have a particularly optimistic outlook about Charles' future; his last progress note prior to his release suggests that their expectations were very limited. "Although Charles' delusional ideas will probably always remain in the background, his behavior and manner at present are similar to what they were before his conditional discharge, and he should be all right for several months at least." On May 1, 1986, Charles was discharged from New Hampshire Hospital. The staff evidently anticipated his return. This cycling in and out of hospitals, a result of the push toward deinstitutionalization, is known in the mental health community as "the revolving door."

In October 1986, my father wrote the words that I would read at his funeral: "No matter how adverse the circumstances, there is never any reason to give up." He had not let his second hospitalization in six months deter him from trying to find work and move beyond the designation "schizophrenic." Earlier that month, with his encouragement, his treatment team had forwarded some of his recent writing on Analytic Space to local universities for evaluation. His progress notes recorded the results. "It has been questioned periodically whether the material that Mr. Lachenmeyer works on is intelligent material or a result of psychotic thinking. Recently, much of his work was verified as being legitimate by sociology professors at some local colleges." My father may have had this makeshift peer review in mind when he wrote to me. Whatever hopes he had that the positive feedback might lead to a teaching position, however, were not borne out. When he met with the professors who had reviewed his work, he was unable to convince them to recommend him for a part-time position as a receptionist or file clerk, let alone as a professor.

When Charles told Englund about the interviews, he seemed frustrated by the lack of clarity in his thought processes. Englund suspected that Charles was afraid that his occasional confusion might have been evident during interviews. "Charles was a very intelligent and verbal person with quick responses and associations, but I think at times he felt like he was not being intelligent in the way that he was communicating. The way I saw it, what was going on was that he maintained his memory and his vocabulary, and the disorder seemed to affect the way he was able to structure his thoughts. To the extent that he was aware of his cognitive difficulties, he would have attributed them to the actions of his medications or his persecutors rather than schizophrenia."

Charles continued to apply for teaching positions and to work on his independent research, but the recurring pressures and disappointments took their toll. During his weekly meetings with Englund, he began to fixate more and more on Thought Control and became increasingly agitated and paranoid. Then in April 1987, Charles accused Englund of being part of the conspiracy and refused to meet with him anymore. After trying without success for several weeks to reach him by telephone, Englund attempted a home visit, but Charles refused to answer the door. Englund returned again the following week. Charles opened the door, but would not take off the chain. When Englund attempted to reach through the crack in the door, Charles abruptly slammed it shut with his shoulder, almost catching Englund's arm in the process. Ten years later, Englund's face still registered his disappointment and frustration when he recalled their last encounter. "I wanted to reach Charles, whoever he was—his core person—but I couldn't. His disorder stood between us. I had a lot of respect for Charles. I saw him as a heroic figure. He was fighting a losing battle against a disease, and he did it with an unusual degree of dignity and self-respect."

The next day, Charles was picked up by the police and returned to New Hampshire Hospital. One month later, he was released again. Hoping the job prospects would be better, he moved to Manchester, the largest city in the state. His case was transferred to the Mental Health Center of Manchester and he was assigned a new treatment team. He had no luck finding work, but continued to send out query letters every day.

That December, I turned eighteen. I was a freshman in college, confused and miserable, trying to adapt to the social climate of dorm life. For only the second time since the divorce, my father had not sent me a birthday present. (The first time was during his sixteen-month hospitalization.) I cried, thinking that he had forgotten my birthday, and recalled with a sudden appreciation the eclectic array of birthday presents he had given me over the years: a full set of wooden table settings; an encyclopedia of art; a table lamp in the shape of a bald eagle; a large cast iron kettle; a set of drafting pens; a field guide to animal tracks; a book on mythical monsters. I sat up all night writing and rewriting a long letter to him—my first in over a year—telling him all about college life and letting him know how much I missed him. I also sent him a small handmade chapbook of the poetry I had written in high school, which included a bad poem about a transient called "Bag Lady at 104th and Broadway."

The day after my birthday I received my father's present in the mail—a copy of his favorite book, *The Collected Plays of Eugene O'Neill*. He had not forgotten my birthday after all. My father responded to my letter the following week with a long nostalgic letter of his own, filled with reminiscences about his life at eighteen—William and Mary and the discovery of women and sociology—not to mention a touch of literary criticism. "Your poems—the only line I do not think belongs there is the one about the bees. It trivializes what you have to say!" He also expressed some fatherly concern. "I was a little disturbed at several things in your letter. 'Not too many close friends.' I know it sounds trite, but from hard experience you must learn to take people as they are, not as you want them to be. One of my major problems over the years was being too critical of people when we all have the same concerns. 'Uncomfortable with your environment.' I do not know what you are referring to, but when I was your age I went through the same thing. It will pass!"

Thus began our only year of truly active correspondence. In 1988, when I was eighteen and my father was forty-five, we came closest to recovering what we had lost eight years earlier. I enjoyed his letters and wrote back regularly for the first time since the divorce, but I could not stop myself from searching every letter for some indication that he was still symptomatic. There was none. The letters back and forth were a kind of courtship, an earnest attempt to reinvest our relationship with some of the meaning it had once had. We focused on the best years and avoided any subjects that might have caused either of us to withdraw.

My father: "It has been a very long time, but even though we have been separated for so long it has not diminished my love for you. If anything I live too much in the past. To me you are still an eleven-year-old boy. But you are a man now. When we were separated it was as if someone had yanked out my heart. My memories always go back to our bike rides together, our fishing trips, our walks with Georgie, the movies, the dinners out, and so on. I regret very much the past eight years. But enough of that. If we keep writing we should at least be able to hold the Father-Son thing together."
Me: "I remember watching monster movies together, walking Georgie, going crabbing and fishing, trying to do chin ups with you in the garage, hatching plans, searching for finds. I must admit such memories are scattered, but my feelings are not: you are very important to me. It is important to me that things go well for you, and that we keep writing."

One year later, in the fall of 1988, my father and I were still writing to each other regularly. He kept me updated on his job efforts and described his work on Analytic Space. I told him about my classes and dating adventures. We discussed our shared interests in psychology and philosophy—my intended major—and even recommended books to each other: my father, classics that I had never heard of; me, new authors that my father was not familiar with because he had been away from academia for so long.

Then in January 1989 my father called to tell me that he would be in New York for the marriage of his brother-cousin, Joel, and asked if I wanted to see him. I told him that I needed to think about it. The idea of a reunion after so long scared me more than it should have. If my father still thought of me in some respects as his eleven-year-old son, I still thought of him as the crazy father who left obscene and threatening messages on the answering machine in Pelham. It was with these memories foremost in mind that I sat down and wrote him a letter, asking him openly for the first time about his diagnosis. In bringing the subject up, I wanted to have everything out in the open prior to our reunion. In effect, however, what I was doing was asking him a terrible and naïve question: was he still crazy?

My father responded by sending me a detailed letter that described everything that had happened to him over the previous ten years—including his hospitalizations at New Hampshire Hospital—from the vantage point of his delusional system. "What I am about to write is to be held in the strictest confidence. I have not told another soul these things except when I was first admitted to the hospital, for which (and because I

refused 'treatment') I spent 16 months incarcer-
ated . . ." What followed was an eight-page chronology
of the various phases of the conspiracy. My father
began and ended the letter by both denying that he was
mentally ill and reproaching me for blaming him for
his illness—words that bite deep even a decade later:

> *Dearest Nathaniel,*
> *Just received your letter. Even if I was a paranoid*
> *schizophrenic, which I am not, where is your charity?*
> *Such a condition is brought on by medical/social*
> *factors over which one does not have control and it is*
> *incumbent not to blame the victim . . .*

> *. . . Anyway, at no point was I delusional, hearing*
> *voices or anything like that. And even if it were all*
> *in my imagination, which it is not, you have a hell*
> *of a nerve turning your back on your father. I am*
> *not supposed to say this—I have been counseled*
> *against it—but you sound like an arrogant little*
> *shit who needs his behind warmed.*

> *Love, Dad.*

I was nineteen when I first read those words—a
young nineteen. I knew that my father was in a great
deal of pain when he wrote the letter—tear stains had
bled the ink in parts—but I focused on the words themselves rather than on the context in which they were

written. He was right; I was an arrogant little shit. I responded with a curt note in which I broke off all contact, explaining, "I can't live in your world; you can't live in mine." I did not understand at the time that my father's denial that he had schizophrenia was a feature of the disorder itself. Nor did I understand that my bringing up his diagnosis put me on the side of his persecutors, who, he believed, were doing everything in their power to convince him that he was ill. My question had driven home the fact that he had failed to accomplish what he had described on the answering machine tape from 1983 as his primary goal in self-publishing his newsletters. "I will be doing that directly for my son, so that you people cannot fool with pictorial representations and rewriting history."

When I think now about my decision to cut off contact with my father, I remember the words that John Englund used to describe the importance of my role in his life. "His relationship with you was the one place in his life where he felt hope and connection. I felt that if you and he did not maintain contact, that that would be severing the last wire for him." I severed that wire without thinking about the consequences for my father, and did not look back until it was too late. I should have realized that, regardless of the content of his delusional system, my father needed sustained social contact as much as everyone else. I should have asked myself, if he could not count on his son for that, who would he be able to count on? For his part, my father continued to write to me, sporadically updating me on his life and expressing the hope that we might still be able to pick up where we had left off. He refused to give up on our relationship, despite my turning my back on him and despite the suffering he had endured.

After leaving John Englund, I drove directly to Manchester and interviewed members of his treatment team at the Mental Health Center of Manchester. Between his third release from New Hampshire Hospital and January 1989 my father was bounced from case manager to case manager. Undervalued and poorly compensated, case managers tend to burn out quickly and move on to other work. Around the time that I broke off contact with my father, his case was transferred to Diane DiStaso. Small, tough, and direct, she immediately put me at ease by letting me know that the circumstances of our meeting were not as unfamiliar to her as they were to me; it was not the first time a family member had come to her to learn about a mentally ill relative after having been informed that they had died. What she had to tell me about my father made me wish even more, if possible, that I had not cut off contact with him when I did.

In November 1989, Charles disappeared. After he missed two meetings, DiStaso became concerned and attempted a home visit. There, she found Charles' mailbox cluttered with rejection letters from universities.

Afraid that he had moved without notifying his treatment team, she called Clifford, who reported that Charles had called him in late October and said, "I am going to teach sailors in the navy sociology." DiStaso was convinced that this improbable statement was the product of delusional thinking and that Charles had left Manchester and probably New Hampshire for points unknown, perhaps making good on his perennial threat to move back to Canada.

What Charles had told his cousin, however, was true. The month before, Charles' diligent search for a teaching position had finally yielded tangible results. His first and only teaching position in a decade took him thousands of miles away from New Hampshire. From November 27, 1989, through January 12, 1990, Charles taught two psychology courses and two sociology courses to crew members on board the guided missile frigate USS *Simpson* while it was escorting US-flagged and neutral shipping in the Persian Gulf during Desert Storm. The position, offered through Central Texas College in Killeen, Texas, in conjunction with the US Navy, was evidence of the great lengths to which Charles had gone in his effort to find a teaching position during the previous ten years.

Charles was hired on the strength of his college and graduate school transcripts and of his teaching record in the 1970s. He accounted for the ten-year gap in his résumé by reviving on paper the Institute for the Analysis, Evaluation, and Design of Human Action, which he described as a publishing and consulting company with an international clientele. He listed his salary as director at $30,000 per year and explained that he was looking for work because he had sold the Institute the previous year. Charles received government approval for security clearance and was flown to the Persian Gulf on November 25, 1989. His pay, $810 per course—a total of $3,240—represented a 33 percent increase in his annual income.

Charles returned to Manchester at the end of January. When he called Diane DiStaso and told her where he had been, she called the US Navy, expecting there to be no record of a Charles Lachenmeyer having taught on the USS *Simpson*. She was surprised to learn that he had, in fact, taught four courses at once, and by all accounts had done a very good job. The stress of teaching again for the first time since the onset of his disorder had apparently not affected his performance; nor had his having gone without medication since October. The significance of this was not lost on Charles. DiStaso recorded in his progress notes at the time, "Charles feels he has proven himself in the occupational and social areas of his life on this trip and now would like to continue to seek out employment and make money." On the strength of his accomplishment, Charles requested and was given a trial reduction in his dosage of Haloperidol. The treatment team's goal was to find a dosage low enough to minimize the side effects of the medication, which were still in evidence, but not low enough to cause a relapse.

1989 was Charles' best year since being diagnosed with paranoid schizophrenia from the perspective not only of professional accomplishment but also of the clarity of his thought processes. It was during this period of relative stability that he for the first—and last—time expressed a degree of awareness about his disorder. His progress notes suggest that although he still denied the diagnosis of paranoid schizophrenia and the efficacy of the medication, he did acknowledge having some cognitive difficulties. "Charles feels a need to have counseling around issues of differentiating reality from nonreality. He says he is interested in finding the determining point where thoughts go from being rational to irrational. He also reports obtaining a new perspective of self and illness by focusing on delusions as beliefs. When pressed on his perspective, he does not elaborate." Twenty-five years after working as an attendant at Eastern State Hospital, Charles again appeared to be attempting to "develop a new point of view toward mental illness." Now, however, he was both researcher and experimental subject, and much more—his entire future—was at stake.

Charles' statement begs the question, what new perspective could he gain by redefining his delusions as beliefs? One possible answer stems from the observation that a person suffering from paranoid schizophrenia can seldom be convinced that his delusions *are* delusions; that is, that they are *false* beliefs. Everything he experiences through the prism of his disorder tells him that his beliefs are true. If someone tries to prove that they are false, he will naturally counter with his experiences to the contrary and dismiss those efforts as reflecting, at best, ignorance and, at worst, conspiratorial deceit. (After all, how else can he explain their inability to understand what is so self-evident to him?) In the process, his delusional system may become more fixed and immutable. If the person with schizophrenia can be encouraged to look at his delusions as *beliefs*, however, without reference to truth or falsehood, it will become easier for him to accept that other people can have opposing beliefs and not necessarily be part of a coordinated conspiracy. It might even make it easier for him, over time, to abandon his beliefs in favor of beliefs that enjoy greater social acceptance.

Redefining delusions as beliefs is an exercise in tolerance that, in order to have a sustained beneficial effect on the person with the disorder, would have to be extended to include the people with whom he comes in contact. The public would need to be taught to be more tolerant of the conceptual and behavioral aberrations associated with schizophrenia in much the same way that we are taught from an early age to respect differences in religious belief and practice. When I broke off contact with my father I was demonstrating exactly this kind of intolerance. To argue that our worldviews were incompatible, and, therefore, that I could have nothing to do with him, was prejudice masquerading as logic; there is no one who does not spend large parts of each day surrounded by people who have beliefs that are incompatible with their own. Greater tolerance of the person with schizophrenia's belief system would greatly reduce their stress level, making it easier for them to live in *our* world as they struggle to make sense of *their* world, instead of forcing them to experience ever-increasing marginalization as the outsider.

As Charles continued to struggle to put his life back together and to arrive at a perspective on his aberrant thoughts that would allow him to coexist peacefully with the broader social world, he learned that his time might be running out. His progress notes from July 1991 record, "Mr. Lachenmeyer had a complete physical recently and evidence was found that he may have suffered a minor heart attack, without knowledge of it." Ten years of constant and debilitating stress attempting to cope with his disorder had undoubtedly contributed to his deteriorating health. The unhealthy lifestyle schizophrenia tends to impose on its victims probably also played a role.

There is, for example, an unusually high prevalence of smoking among people with schizophrenia. Charles was no exception. According to DiStaso, he smoked more cigarettes than any other client she had ever had—so many that both of his hands were permanently stained yellow from the nicotine. Seventy-five to ninety percent of people with schizophrenia smoke, more than three times the national average. There is evidence that smoking alleviates some of the symptoms of schizophrenia, and so may be a form of self-medication. (There is also evidence to suggest that nicotine interferes with the efficacy of antipsychotic medication.) Once addicted to nicotine, it is even harder for people with schizophrenia to quit smoking than it is for the general population because nicotine withdrawal can cause a temporary worsening of their symptoms. As a result, they have a much higher risk of developing diseases linked to smoking, such as heart disease, lung cancer, and emphysema.

On Christmas Day, 1991, my father, perhaps reflecting on his failing physical health, wrote me a letter in which he revisited my decision to cut off contact with the following assertion. "It is provable that the decision to absolutely exclude another in self-perpetuation produces no understanding and attenuated knowing, and is subject to the sustainability of a contradiction in which you absolutely exclude yourself." My father wanted a chance to renew our relationship. He wanted it badly enough that he attempted to prove its logical necessity, using Analytic Space. Rereading his letter after his death, I realized that he had been right: logical necessity aside, my exclusion of him *had* led to self-exclusion, first, because it entailed the destruction of my identity as my father's son, and, second, because my attendant feelings of guilt interfered with my ability to define myself as anything else.

In the months following his physical, Charles began to show increased signs of the involuntary writhing movements known as Tardive Dyskinesia. After several further trial reductions in the dosage of his medication, in the spring of 1992 his treatment team realized that they had gone too far. His delusions once again began to take center stage in his life. Charles wrote letter after letter to his treatment team decrying their participation in a dramatic intensification of Thought Control. In the first of a series of letters to his legal guardian protesting the guardianship, Charles logged the day on which it had all begun. "As you know, as of 1/15/92 to the present my persecutors have reemerged mostly with a pattern of vehicular harassment which includes the police of Manchester." In a letter to DiStaso in which he announced his refusal to attend any future weekly meetings or accept any more medication, he set out to deny all prior statements he had made that suggested that he had questioned his own sanity. "I consider all past statements about mental stability that may have found their way into my chart to have been made under duress." Presumably, he had in mind, among other things, the new perspective he had obtained by focusing on delusions as beliefs.

Charles once again believed wholeheartedly that his

challenge was to defend his sanity in the face of his persecutors' coordinated efforts to have him labeled insane. He abandoned his attempt to develop a new point of view toward mental illness. He also left behind his independent research on Analytic Space. For the first time since 1983, Charles devoted himself exclusively to protesting Thought Control. He again spent what little money he had on mass mailings intended to expose to the world the injustice of the experiment to which he had been subjected. Reflecting his diminished resources, his mailings no longer consisted of stand-alone, self-published newsletters; they now consisted of a single stapled packet of photocopied letters which he had written to individual co-conspirators.

I had received a copy of the packet back in 1992, but never read through all the letters it contained. I first read the entire collection when I saw the packet again while looking through my father's file at the Mental Health Center of Manchester, after interviewing Diane DiStaso. I was shocked to discover, in between letters to the President of the United States and the editor of the *New York Times*, a letter to me, which I had not seen in 1992. The beginning of the letter made clear that in my father's mind I had finally joined the ranks of co-conspirator. Given that he did not know that he was ill, how else could he account for my stubborn refusal to renew contact? "Nathaniel, As you now know and understand everything I wrote you before describing my eleven years of torment is true. As you can see from the enclosed the work becomes stronger each month. Maybe my fine friend you can meet such challenges and perfect your craft."

In the body of the letter and in the other letters in the packet my father continued his analysis of Thought Control, enumerating the ways his persecutors had used their privileged knowledge of his thoughts and of his past to try to get him to believe that he was mentally ill. For the first and only time, he wrote about his mother's place in their strategy, describing explicitly their attempts to convince him that he was like her. "My mother's tendency to 'keep things in' and burst out in tirades has for years been publicly flaunted under the label 'paranoia.' 'Your mother is going to die' has been the publicly used rallying cry for a systematic attempt to rid me of the 'demons' she was supposed to have possessed. For the last three months, they have even inserted a simulation of her voice into my head—the culmination of a series of technological transformations."

Here, at last, buried in a forgotten file in the Mental Health Center of Manchester, was the answer to the question I had been asking myself since my first visit to Burlington: why had my father heard his mother's voice speaking to him twenty years after her death while homeless on the streets of Burlington? Viewed from my father's perspective, the answer was that his persecutors had inserted his mother's voice into his head to try to break him down, to try to get him to finally admit defeat and accept the diagnosis of schizophrenia. He was not being haunted by his mother's ghost in Leunigs Restaurant in Burlington in 1993; he was being haunted, as he had been for more than ten years, by the machinations of Thought Control.

Viewed independently of my father's delusional system, all that can be said is that the fact that he specifically heard his mother's voice was not surprising and was probably not arbitrary. She was, after all, the central influence in his life. But this is not what guaranteed his mother playing such a key role in his delusional system. Grounded by the belief that he was not mentally ill, my father's delusional system had to account for the irony that he had been diagnosed with a disorder which, twenty years earlier, he had predicted he would develop as a result of how she raised him.

In light of Charles' correspondence, and after repeated, failed attempts to convince him to return to the mental health center, his treatment team decided on October 22, 1992, to revoke his conditional discharge and send him back to New Hampshire Hospital. They discovered, however, when they arrived at his apartment with a police escort, that he had anticipated their decision and moved out at the beginning of the month, leaving no forwarding address. Charles was determined not to return to the state hospital a fourth time. After living for ten years in New Hampshire, he had taken to heart the state's motto, emblazoned on every New Hampshire license plate— LIVE FREE OR DIE.

Part Three

When I asked him if he thought he

had a mental illness, he said that he

did and that his mental illness was

"love of life and humanity."

—Excerpt from a psychiatric evaluation
of my father conducted at Vermont
State Hospital, February 1994

Chapter 8

The
Stranger

It was January 1997. I was back in Burlington, Vermont, my fingers again touching the old photograph of my father and me taken in better times. Standing on Church Street on a cold and gray winter day, I remembered one of the more rash ideas that had come to me after my first visit to Burlington: I had thought seriously about growing a beard and moving there to experience life as a transient. It had seemed like that might be the best way to learn about my father's life on the street, until it dawned on me that that would have been confusing masochism with research. The embarrassment I felt recalling my aborted plan stayed with me as I walked in the direction of the white-steepled church at the top of Church Street. In a self-conscious attempt at closure I sat on the same bench I had sat on a year before and looked into Leunigs Restaurant, wondering if I would see my father's successor drinking beer and eating eggs and watching me watching him. I saw the silhouettes of customers—people sitting alone, couples, and families—but no one who appeared homeless.

I had returned to Burlington as myself—a son trying to understand the arc of his father's life. I was here to talk to the handful of people who had witnessed my father's transformation into the ultimate outsider: the transient. It occurred to me that my father had probably sat on the same bench four years earlier in the uniform of the transient, watching some of the same people walk by. I was beginning to see Burlington through his eyes. The Marketplace was Colonial Williamsburg transplanted to Vermont: an elaborate stage set constructed to look like a modest late-twentieth-century city, where actors choreographed their actions and conversations to comment on and control my father's private thoughts. I was struck by the irony that his disorder, which was responsible for his near-total isolation, had also convinced him that he was the central figure in a social experiment that involved tens of thousands of people. Although the involuntary nature of the experiment and the unwillingness of the conspirators to acknowledge its existence must have tormented my father, his perspective did allow him a degree of hope; there was still the possibility that everything could reverse itself suddenly and dramatically, *if* he could convince his persecutors to end the experiment and restore him to his former station in life.

I spent the day walking up and down the Marketplace, showing store owners and employees the photograph of my father, asking them if they remembered someone whom I knew looked almost nothing like the man in the picture. The answer was almost always the same. "Maybe. He looks familiar, but I can't really say." There were a lot of homeless people in Burlington, but almost no one knew any of their names or anything about them, except that they were dirty and smelled bad and that many of them acted strangely. They were a nuisance, a blight on the Marketplace. I could not resent their perspective. If I had been confused enough and scared enough by my father's behavior at better points in his life to turn my back on him and his suffering, how could I blame anyone else for their indifference? Circumstances had never forced them to try to understand schizophrenia or the idea that the homeless have a past not unlike their own.

That evening, I walked to the Way Station, a forty-bed emergency homeless shelter located at 187 Church Street, several blocks south of the Marketplace. I arrived a few minutes before it opened for the night and waited in line with Burlington's homeless. I showed several of them the photograph, but their response was the same as that of their more fortunate counterparts. His description reminded them of someone who had stayed at the shelter a few years back, but transients come and go; there was no way to be sure. There was nothing else to say. The line continued to grow, extending from the front door almost to the curb. I felt conspicuous, the only false link in a chain of suffering and misfortune. While I waited, I went over in my head what I had learned from my father's file at the Mental Health Center of Manchester about how he became homeless.

Upon arrival in Burlington in October of 1992, Charles rented a small efficiency in a communal boardinghouse for $325 per month. He did everything he could to prevent his treatment team from finding him. Not only did he not tell anyone in Manchester where he was, he did not even give the post office his forwarding address, sacrificing any chance of a reply to his query letters to universities. His only connection to Manchester was the local Social Security office; he had to give them his new address, so that they could forward his $604 a month in SSI benefits. He arranged to have his only other source of income, his pension from his years of teaching at Hunter, $225 a month, wired directly to the Howard Bank in Burlington, where he had opened an account.

Charles underestimated his treatment team's resolve. After calling the Social Security office and discovering that Charles had moved to Burlington, his legal guardian did something unexpected and unorthodox; he applied for and received from the Social Security office "representative payee status" over Charles. This meant that his SSI benefits—63% of his income— began to be rerouted to the Office of Public Guardian, where they were held in his name. Charles' guardianship, as defined by the courts, did not place any restrictions on his finances. In securing representative payee status over Charles, his legal guardian effectively extended the guardianship to include his finances without having to go through the court system. His goal was to use his representative payee status as leverage to try to convince Charles to return to Manchester, where he had a prior relationship with local mental health agencies, or to agree to meet with a case manager in Burlington and resume taking his medication.

If Charles had underestimated his legal guardian's determination, his legal guardian had overestimated the extent to which Charles was able to think and act independently of the delusional system his disorder imposed on him. He had not capitulated at all during the previous eleven years of persecution; he was not about to start now. The legal guardian's maneuver confirmed, in Charles' mind, his former treatment team's involvement in the experiment he was trying so hard to escape. It is easy to imagine how Charles would have interpreted his actions. His persecutors were punishing him for his successful escape from a return to the role of prisoner. They were withholding his SSI benefits to try to make freedom a less attractive option for Charles than imprisonment. Charles' challenge was to not surrender, to dig in and maintain his freedom at all costs, despite the dangerous escalation in the experiment.

Charles knew that he had to regain control of his SSI benefits immediately or face eviction. He started firing off letters of protest to the probate court in New

Hampshire, contesting the guardianship. At the same time Charles sent more subdued letters to the guardian informing him of his efforts to find work locally, and entreating him to forward his SSI checks. His legal guardian held firm, however, refusing to release even a portion of his funds until he agreed to seek treatment. Emboldened by long-standing rumors that Charles had a source of income other than SSI, he incorrectly assumed that it was significant enough that the absence of his SSI benefits would not jeopardize his ability to pay room and board.

While Charles waited to hear from the probate court, he redoubled his efforts to find work in an attempt to reduce his dependency on disability benefits. Toward this end, he took a calculated risk with his limited resources and spent two hundred dollars on a mass mailing of his résumé and a summary of his current research to dozens of companies and universities throughout New England. Charles managed to stay at 16 Hickock Place through the winter, but by the beginning of March his legal guardian still had not forwarded any checks and his job search had not yielded any results. As Charles fell further and further behind on his rent and his situation grew more desperate, his appearance and behavior became increasingly bizarre. He stopped maintaining his hygiene. Neighbors complained about shouting coming from his room at all hours. They suspected him of going through their mail and were made uncomfortable by the way he glared at them from his window, which faced the street. In short, he was exhibiting the same kind of behavior he had exhibited seven years earlier in Manchester. Finally, on March 17, 1993, Charles was evicted from 16 Hickock Place—penniless and floridly delusional. That his transformation into the transient was so sudden underscores what a fine line he had been walking all the years after onset.

At seven o'clock the door to the shelter opened. I followed the others in and introduced myself to the director, who was signing the night's residents into the daily log book. A bearded, middle-aged man in his forties, he had a weathered face, a gravelly voice, and the bitter appreciation of irony that comes from extended exposure to hard times—his own and other people's. After he had checked in the night's residents, we went into his office, a tiny room half-lit by bare fluorescent lights. The director began by explaining the setup. Prospective residents had to meet several requirements to be able to stay at the Way Station: they had to be homeless; they had to treat the staff and their fellow boarders with respect; they had to maintain their hygiene; and they had to demonstrate that they were actively trying to improve their situation. Residents were allowed to stay a maximum of ninety nights a year at the shelter and to use the Way Station as their permanent mailing address, which I realized must have given my father the faint hope that he might still receive a job offer in response to his mass mailing—a last minute reprieve from a life on the street.

After checking his files, the director told me that Charles showed up at the Way Station for the first time on the evening of March 17, 1993—the same day he was kicked out of his apartment. He recalled that Charles was not humbled in the least by his change in circumstances, and found him to be confrontational and "a little prickly." His "prickliness" manifested itself early on, most noticeably in his refusal to improve his hygiene. Poor hygiene is common among people suffering from schizophrenia, irrespective of their living conditions. It is a manifestation of a hallmark symptom of schizophrenia—grossly disorganized behavior—and is something over which they have little control. The fact that maintaining good hygiene was one of the shelter's requirements is certainly understandable, but it is also indicative of how people with schizophrenia are at a disadvantage even in the context of a homeless shelter.

During the spring and summer of 1993, Charles did not sleep at the Way Station often enough for his poor hygiene to threaten his status as a resident. When the director asked him at one point where he stayed at night when he was not at the Way Station, Charles told him "the subway," and explained that he was saving the majority of his ninety nights for later in the year in case he was still homeless when winter arrived. Charles' confrontational style and his inability to meet the demands set by the staff did not bode well, however, for his future at the shelter.

At the end of our conversation the director mentioned that there was someone staying at the Way Station that night who might remember my father. I felt self-conscious as I entered the sleeping area, a harshly lit square where twenty bunk beds were arranged in rows, each with two numbers neatly stenciled on the side. Forty men were in various states of undress—transients stepping out of their uniform, becoming recognizable as individuals. The beds themselves conveyed their occupants' distinctive personalities; most were adorned, many with objects that were obviously retrieved from someone's trash—mangy stuffed animals, small piles of water-damaged books or out-of-date magazines, a chipped ashtray, a broken mug. I introduced myself to the transient in bed no. 22, a bearded transient in his early forties whose appearance fit the stereotype of a Vermont woodsman.

After we shook hands and he offered me his condolences on my father's death, we decided to talk outside on Church Street where we would not disturb the other residents. It was cold and the stars were bright over our heads. The transient told me that the low temperature that night was expected to be three degrees. He explained that there was one thing in particular he wanted to tell me. "What happened to your father was a meltdown that I as a human being was not prepared to watch. I could not watch the man go all the way down. I want you to know that I did *not* know that you existed. If I knew that you existed, I would have dropped in a dime and called you up."

The transient naturally assumed that I had had no knowledge of my father's predicament. I did not tell him that my father had written his last letter to me only five months before he became homeless. A veiled plea for financial assistance, the tone of the letter made clear that my father did not hold out much hope that he could depend on me. "Immediate need: $325.00. Exploring possibility of raising 250K. Initiatives underway for position or funding from Australia to Saudi Arabia." A similar effort had yielded results with Clifford. "PS Clifford has invested $300 and my former landlord $1,500." The fifteen hundred dollars "invested" by the landlord in New Hampshire was the back rent my father owed at the time he left the state. For my part, I did not see the desperation behind the distant tone and ignored my father's entreaty.

Now, four years after receiving that letter, I was standing on Church Street, asking another Burlington transient to describe his first encounter with my father. He remembered it well. On a mild day in April 1993 he was sitting on a bench by the fountain in the center of City Hall Park. The only other person in the park at that moment was a tall, unkempt stranger walking along one of the diagonal paths leading to the fountain. The stranger wore a soiled blue sports jacket, a white oxford shirt, dirty slacks, and a decent pair of shoes.

His hair was long and unruly and his beard was ungroomed. Without breaking his stride, the stranger walked up to the transient and sat down. It was apparent that he wanted company; there were a half-dozen unoccupied benches scattered throughout the park, any of which he could have sat on if he wanted to be alone. Without a word of introduction the stranger started talking, quickly and angrily, outlining a vast conspiracy that included the CIA, the FBI, AT&T, the Air Force, and his landlord. "When I first met Charles he had his odd way and stuff but when you talked to him you understood this was an educated man, a man of substance, and a man who could talk. Then he would go into a—I do not know if it is considered a delusion or what—but he would go into that and then he would come back and visit me again. He was thinking that people were always watching him, always wanting to grab him, always wanting to *do something to him* that he did not want done."

The transient had been homeless for years and was well-versed in the symptoms of paranoid schizophrenia. Many of the other homeless in Burlington whom he counted among his friends, he explained, expressed delusions that were similar to my father's. "I had heard all this before. I am sitting there and I am shaking my head, 'Yes, yes, the CIA or the FBI or the Internal Revenue Service, all this and all that.' I would listen to him the way he would say it and I would think to myself this might possibly be true. But I would say to him, 'You got to go through channels. You got to go to people to help them help you sort this out.' He would not listen to that."

The transient and Charles became cautious friends during the spring of 1993, despite their differences in perspective. From time to time Charles would sit down on a bench next to him in City Hall Park or on the Marketplace, bum a cigarette, and talk about the conspiracy that had ruined his life. Burlington was small enough that the transient often saw Charles around town in between his delusional monologues. In some respects, little had changed in Charles' life. The pattern of his day was still determined largely by his need for structure and by his desire for social contact. Most mornings he walked to the Fletcher Free Library, one block east of Church Street on College Street, and read the *Burlington Free Press* and the *New York Times*. Although his circumstances prevented him from continuing his job search, he was still writing; he was often seen scribbling furiously in a spiral notebook. It is likely that Charles was continuing his indictment of Thought Control, which he had returned to after stopping his medication, but he never showed anyone what he was working on. He spent most of each afternoon and evening hanging out in restaurants on the Marketplace, drinking one cup of coffee after another, chain-smoking, and watching Burlington pace back and forth in front of him. At night he sat on one of the benches on Church Street, and, ignoring the cold—the average low in April in Burlington is thirty-four degrees—and the occasional passerby, slept fitfully.

Struggling to cope with the stress of his situation and the return in full force of Thought Control, Charles was drinking more alcohol than ever before. Another former Way Station resident who had since moved on once told the transient that he had visited Charles before he was evicted from his room and that even then "you had to push your way into his room to open the door because of the quarts of beer in there." The transient was not surprised; most of the homeless he knew, whether they suffered from schizophrenia or not, drank in an effort to make their lives more bearable. At the beginning of each month, when Charles received his pension check, he would hang out in local bars after the restaurants closed. By the start of the summer, however, his increasingly poor hygiene and his penchant for talking to himself had led the bars to close their doors to him, forcing him to drink beer surreptitiously on the street.

Over the spring and summer my father became a fixture on the Marketplace. Except for brief conversations with bartenders and waitresses who dismissed him as "weird" and a "wacko," the only opportunity he had to socialize with people—to hear voices that could compete for attention with the voices raging in his head—was when he sat next to someone on one of the benches around town, or on the rare occasion when someone sat next to him.

Realizing how important my father's brief conversations with the transient must have been to him, I asked the transient why he stuck around when my father went on and on about the CIA and the FBI. "There are times people have to have somebody around. You know? Maybe I turned my mind off and was not really definitely listening to him, but I could feel that he could feel my presence there, and it helped him. I hope it helped him. I remember one day during the summer, for example, I sat down next to him and he told me that it was his fiftieth birthday *that day*. We spent a little time together on the bench. I know I would not want to be alone on my fiftieth birthday." The transient understood better than I did that what people suffering from schizophrenia need more than anything is sustained social contact.

After shaking the transient's hand and watching the Way Station door close behind him, I stood there and wondered what part my father would have thought his friend had, if any, in the experiment. I wondered if he had reminded my father of our encounter with another transient in Times Square all those years before, or if my father even remembered that day at all. If he did, he probably thought that his persecutors had put him in his path to remind him of that fateful exchange, and what he had lost since then. Or, perhaps, he would have decided that his persecutors had dismissed the transient as too insignificant to co-opt. It occurred to me that the transient, who told me that he worked construction whenever there was a building going up in town, matched the description my father had given thirty years earlier of the "toothless people," the day laborers in Dexter, Maine. My father may have thought that his persecutors had tapped his memory of Dexter, Maine, and intentionally put the transient in his path to remind him of the dangers of romanticizing the role of the outsider. One thing was clear: my father's paranoid conception of Thought Control would have obliged him to engage in the same speculation that I was attempting, and that speculation meant that even in the company of a friend he was fundamentally alone and on his guard.

Temperatures in September in Burlington are mild enough—the average high is sixty-nine degrees; the average low is forty-nine degrees—that my father was still able to sit on the park benches on the Marketplace and in City Hall Park and have reason to hope that from time to time someone from the world he used to inhabit would sit down next to him to enjoy the weather. Someone did. I would never have found Jason Palmer if he had not responded to an ad I placed in the *Burlington Free Press* requesting information from anyone who might have known my father. We agreed to meet on the park bench where they had met, a few benches up from Leunigs on Church Street. A twenty-six-year-old English major at the University of Vermont, Jason reminded me a little of myself in the years prior to my father's death—confident, intelligent, and romantic, with an exaggerated faith in the written word and the exchange of ideas.

One afternoon in September 1993, Charles was sitting on a bench on Church Street. He saw Jason walking by, lighting a cigarette, and asked him for one. Several weeks and a handful of cigarettes later, Jason sat down next to Charles and they had their first extended conversation. "He was talking to himself in a rather agitated way. Even though a lot of what he said was nonsensical, it was clear that he was educated and very intelligent. At the end of a long monologue about numbers and people, he said something that stood out in my mind. He said, 'Important things happen only at nine o'clock in the morning and nine o'clock at night.'"

The next time Charles asked him for a cigarette, Jason suggested a trade: a cigarette for an explanation of what he had meant. Charles replied, "You will have to get back to me on that," took the cigarette out of Jason's hand, and walked up Church Street. Charles' composure struck Jason as incongruous and a little amusing, given his circumstances. When Jason saw Charles sitting on a bench on the Marketplace a few days later, he asked him again. "His answer had to do with the laws of probability. He said that it was like pebbles scattered on a beach near the ocean; how many pebbles there are has to do with why important things happen to people at nine o'clock in the morning and nine o'clock at night. It did not make sense to me, but it seemed like it made sense to him."

After that conversation, a modest friendship began to develop between Charles and Jason. Jason soon realized that Charles did not just see himself as a homeless person struggling to survive on the street; it was clear that he felt that his life had a purpose. His reference to when important things happen, the way he looked at people walking by, the fact that he occasionally mentioned his "work," left Jason with the impression that he was trying to figure out how he had gotten to this point in his life.

Before long, Charles started to trust Jason enough to offer him relatively unguarded access to his thought processes. He told him what he had told the transient about the conspiracy and from time to time would even point at someone walking by and explain the role they had in the conspiracy. Jason never disputed or challenged Charles' delusional claims and was happy to listen—in effect, applying Charles' principle of redefining delusions as beliefs. Perhaps sensing this, Charles moved beyond the conspiracy to tell Jason a little about his life and background. "He told me that he had been a professor at one point in time. He said he taught sociology. He said that he learned more in the bars than he did in the classroom."

It was a change in seasons that broke the tentative connection established between professor-turned-transient and student. In Burlington the temperature drops another ten degrees in October. The average high is fifty-seven degrees; the average low thirty-nine. October strips the Marketplace of pedestrians as effectively as it does the leaves from the trees. It is no longer pleasant for people to while away an hour or two sitting on benches. With the cold weather, Charles began to change. His life as a transient, which in the spring and summer months had had some minimal stability, began to fall apart around him. There were fewer and fewer people for him to talk to. Months of eating poorly had left him underweight and severely malnourished. He was so unkempt and dirty that almost no restaurants would agree to serve him, which meant that he was spending more and more time outside in the cold. It is likely that sitting on one of those park benches, there was a single discrete moment when he suddenly realized for the first time that the street might kill him.

The last conversation Jason had with my father took place on a cold day in mid-October. Sitting with Jason on Church Street, I could read the ambivalence in his face; he was unsure how I would respond to what he was about to say. On that particular day my father was walking down the street more quickly than usual, and he seemed very agitated. For the first time, Jason felt afraid of him. He walked up to Jason, towered over him, and announced in an angry voice, "I am writing a book." When Jason asked him what he meant, he explained, "I am writing a book inside my head. The book is being written as I stand here." Then my father began to quote from the book he was writing. " 'These punks in the park, they stole a man's hat. They took his hat, the only thing that kept him warm. They did not need a hat.' " It was clear to Jason that my father was talking about himself, and that this "book" was a record of what his conspirators had done to him.

My father sat down and abruptly changed the subject. For the first time he asked Jason what his name was and how old he was. When Jason answered, my father volunteered that he had a son. That was the first Jason had heard of my existence. The idea shocked him; it seemed inconceivable that the unkempt, soiled transient who spent his days on benches on Church Street was someone's father.

It was both gratifying and harrowing to learn that I was still in my father's thoughts that fall. His last letter to me, in which he had hinted at needing money, was already a year old at that time, buried away in a drawer and forgotten. What my father said next scared us both. "My son had a friend named Jason. My son was down and his friend was up, and when you kill one, you have got to kill them both." Jason had no idea what my father was talking about and did not think that he had actually killed someone, but he decided that he had had enough of the transient for one day. As a spontaneous gesture, before leaving, Jason gave him a copy of a book he was reading—*Damian* by Herman Hesse.

I was silent when Jason finished his story. Hearing my father talk about killing me scared me as much as his talking about killing Jason had scared him. Jason and I took a break from our discussion and watched life on the Marketplace. After a few minutes, a transient passed by close enough for us to smell him, which brought us both back to my father. I asked Jason what happened between them after that encounter. From that point on my father kept his distance. Whenever he saw Jason on the Marketplace he acknowledged him with a nod, but he never again approached him, even to ask for a cigarette. Jason was both relieved and puzzled by his withdrawal. Their friendship, which lasted three months from start to finish, had begun with one riddle and ended with another.

I had learned enough about my father's delusional system to guess what had happened. Already agitated because his hat had been stolen, he was taken aback when Jason asked him about the book he said he was writing in his head. My father had to decide on the spot if Jason already knew about the book or not; was he programmed to ask the question, perhaps, to let my father know that his persecutors were aware of his book, or was he just genuinely curious? When Jason told him his name, then revealed that he was about the same age as me, my father had his answer. When I was growing up in Pelham I played kickball all the time with a boy in my class named Jason, who lived on my block. In my father's world of conspiracies, surrogates, and choreographed scenes, there were no coincidences; he had no choice but to conclude that Jason was intended as a surrogate for me, and that his persecutors had orchestrated their exchanges. My guess was that my father had scared Jason on purpose, after discovering that he was not, as he had hoped, his friend. There are few things as scary as an unkempt madman talking casually about killing his son.

Speculating about what my father may have thought Jason's role in the experiment was brought me back to the transient; and then, back further, to my father having heard his mother's voice while living on the street. I began to see a pattern emerging, to see the experiment as my father must have seen it, when he was the transient. The past was returning en masse to haunt my father on Church Street. Hearing his mother's voice was just one part of a larger plan. The major participants in my father's life had been brought back in the form of surrogates to play on his insecurities about his mental health, and to emphasize what he had lost in his effort to retain his freedom at all costs. My father's response was to once again protest in writing the unethical treatment to which he was being subjected. Now, his means were so limited, however, that he was forced to write without the benefit of paper or pen and to rely entirely on the efficacy of the mind-reading component of Thought Control to reach his audience.

In the fall of 1993 a figure out of my father's past appeared before him on the Marketplace—not a surrogate, an actual person from the days before the onset of schizophrenia. Dr. John Burchard had been teaching psychology at the University of Vermont since 1970. Prior to that, he taught at the University of North Carolina at Chapel Hill and ran an experimental unit at the Murdoch Center for the Retarded at John Ulmstead Hospital in nearby Butner, North Carolina. In 1966, as a graduate student in sociology at Chapel Hill, my father worked under Dr. Burchard at the Murdoch Center. While visiting Chapel Hill in the fall of 1996 I learned that Dr. Burchard was teaching in Burlington at the time that my father was homeless. I met with Dr. Burchard in his office at the University of Vermont after arriving in Burlington and discovered, to both our surprise, that, twenty-seven years later, their paths had crossed again on Church Street, although Dr. Burchard did not recognize his former employee in his current incarnation as the transient.

Homeless on Church Street, Charles did recognize his former employer—and for a brief moment held out the hope that his sudden appearance might herald a change in his fortunes. One afternoon in early October, Dr. Burchard found a hand-delivered letter from Charles sitting in his mailbox at the university. In the letter, written on stationery from the Radisson Hotel in Burlington, Charles reminisced about Chapel Hill and described his subsequent professional accomplishments in detail. He also described his current work activities, but kept his account vague, referring only in the most general terms to his "independent research." He explained that he was passing through Burlington on his way to Canada. Dr. Burchard recalled that there was nothing out of the ordinary about the letter: no trace of paranoia or delusional thinking, no indication that he needed help. The only thing that struck Dr. Burchard as odd at the time was that Charles had not provided any contact information—no address or telephone number—other than the letterhead from the Radisson Hotel.

Charles' predicament was formidable. If Dr. Burchard was not in the employ of his persecutors and his appearance on the Marketplace was a genuine coincidence, then he represented a windfall opportunity. Dr. Burchard was in a unique position to assist Charles in his effort to return to academia. Charles knew that he could not approach him in his current condition if he wanted anything more than change for a cup of coffee; this explained his borrowing stationery from the Radisson Hotel and claiming to be passing through town. The stationery would have given Dr. Burchard a way of contacting Charles, assuming Charles was able to convince a day clerk at the Radisson Hotel to take a message for him. Walking onto campus to drop off the letter, attracting the stares of students and faculty alike, Charles must have felt keenly how far he had fallen in the thirteen years since he had held an academic position at a university.

Even living on the street, my father was still paying the price for his inability to master academic politics.

One of his first published articles was a candid critique of Dr. Burchard's experimental unit at the Murdoch Center, which Dr. Burchard regarded at the time as both a breach of professional etiquette and a personal act of betrayal. Recalling the incident three decades later, Dr. Burchard set the letter aside and did not try to contact him. I can imagine my father checking at the front desk of the Radisson every day or two to see if Dr. Burchard had called and his slow realization that a reply would not be forthcoming. The coincidence would have been hard for anyone to accept, let alone someone whose thought processes invariably interpreted coincidences as evidence of conspiracy. Seeing Dr. Burchard on Church Street must have removed whatever doubt remained in my father's mind that the people walking back and forth in front of him on the Marketplace were designed to resemble people out of his past; that they were part of a coordinated effort to, as he wrote in the first of his delusional newsletters, ridicule and demean him for his past mistakes.

Burlington does not have a subway system. The "subway" where Charles told the Way Station director he spent his nights was part of the ubiquitous international sandwich shop franchise with the yellow decor. Located on Main Street, one-half block east of Church Street, Subway stayed open until four every morning, providing night owls and the homeless with a respite from the cold night air. As cold weather descended on Burlington, Charles spent almost every evening at Subway, nursing a cup of coffee and talking to himself. He was lucky that Amy King, a student at the University of Vermont, worked the evening shift.

I interviewed Amy at Subway late one night in January 1997 over a cup of weak coffee. Dark, young, and timid, she radiated a natural kindness that made me glad that my father had known her when he did. "Charles would come in quite often and sit at this one table and talk to himself for hours. He looked like the sort of person you would encourage to eat something or get some nourishment somehow. He had a really thin, dirty face and sunken-in eyes. He struck me as really unhealthy." Like Jason, Amy was able to see beyond my father's appearance and offer him something material that improved his quality of life, however marginally. Jason had given him cigarettes; Amy gave him coffee. "He started ordering coffee and paying for it. Then a few times he came in and said, 'I do not have any money. Can I have the coffee anyway?' I said, 'Sure,' and poured him a cup. The next time he came in I rang it up, but he just looked at me and smiled and said, 'You know I am not going to pay you.' He was right; I did know. I guess I had started to like him by that point. He made me smile. Pretty soon it got so he would just come in and say, 'Coffee, please,' and I would give him a cup of coffee. I kind of encouraged him to hang out more than he should have."

Charles expressed his appreciation for Amy's generosity by presenting her with a gift. "Occasionally, he would scribble things down on a napkin. One time he gave me what he wrote and said it was to thank me for the coffee. It looked like a formula of numbers and stuff. I thought it was pretty interesting because since he was a homeless person that just wandered the street, you automatically assume that this person has no education or does not know things. It was just sort of the beginning of a hint that he was actually an intelligent person. Even though the formula did not make sense, it had real mathematical kinds of things written down."

It did not take Amy long to notice that sometimes Charles appeared to be talking, not to himself, but to someone else whom only he could hear. She remembered that "He would talk for a while and then sit back like he was listening to someone, and then talk again, like he was responding to what they had just said." Although Charles never volunteered to Amy whom he thought he was talking to, a clue can be found on the walls of Subway itself. The wallpaper at each of the more than eleven thousand Subway shops in the US is covered with old illustrations depicting the history of the New York City subway system. Special emphasis is given to the Brooklyn subway system because the co-founder of Subway, like Charles, was born and raised in Brooklyn. Directly above the table at which Charles always used to sit is a reproduction of an etching of the Graham Avenue Brooklyn City R. R. Co. subway on its route, dated 1898. Under the etching is the following caption:

AT THE BROOKLYN END OF THE BRIDGE
Slightly confusing to a Stranger.

The words could not have played more strongly upon Charles' early fears regarding his mother and her demons had his imagined persecutors composed it themselves—which is undoubtedly how he explained the coincidence to himself. If Amy had asked him to stop talking to himself the way the bartender at Leunigs had, he would probably have also told her that he was talking not to himself but to his mother. Sitting at that table, it is likely that he often traveled back over the bridge to Brooklyn, reliving the years spent in his mother's shadow, living the life of the stranger in his own home, the life of the outsider.

If Amy did not understand Charles—how could she understand a man she knew only as a transient?—she at least did not let his strangeness alienate her. Her tolerance of him helped transform Subway into a safe haven, a place where he could respond to voices and work on his book in relative peace. In fact, Charles apparently saw Amy as helping him with his book. "I was curious about him and why he came in all the time, but I did not want to bother him. Eventually he volunteered. He said, 'You wonder why I am here all the time.' I said, 'Sure.' He said that he was working on a book. He told me he especially enjoyed working with me because we got a lot of good things done together. I did not know what he meant, but it was kind of flattering."

I knew by then that the key to understanding how Amy could have helped my father with his book was the question: who was Amy meant to represent in his past? The answer was provided by Amy's manager at Subway, who told me that my father had confided to her one day that Amy reminded him of his ex-wife—my mother— who had helped edit both of his books in the early 1970s. He never told Amy this himself, probably out of fear that he would scare away one of his few remaining friends in the world. If Amy was a surrogate for my mother, it seemed that she represented her in the innocent years, prior to the intrusion of the conspiracy. Strangely, Amy did resemble my mother in her youth: the shape of her face was similar; she wore her hair the same; and she had a gentleness about her that my mother had in photographs of her at Amy's age.

One evening in late October, Charles took his usual table at Subway. From where he was sitting he was able to look out the window at Main Street and watch the first snowfall of the season. After asking Amy for a refill, he told her a story straight out of urban folklore—the eccentric millionaire dressed in rags who reveals his real identity to the first person who shows him kindness. Appearances to the contrary notwithstanding, Charles claimed that he was not homeless; he said that he owned a spacious, comfortable apartment overlooking the Marketplace. He also owned Subway and most of the other restaurants in downtown Burlington. He even owned the 256-room Radisson Hotel overlooking Lake Champlain—the hotel where I was staying while in Burlington. Amy recalled, "He told me that he was having a big Thanksgiving dinner with his wife and son, whom he had not seen in years, at his hotel, the Radisson, and he invited me to come and to invite my family if I liked. I thanked him, but told him that we always celebrated at home."

Sitting at his table that night, watching the snow cover the stage set called Burlington, Charles had received a sign—perhaps the snow itself—that the persecution was finally going to end and that everything that had been taken from him would be returned. He apparently believed that he would be reunited with his wife and son. He believed that he again had a home of his own. He even believed—he may even have heard voices telling him—that he had been made a gift of the various scenes of his final struggle—Leunigs, Subway, the Radisson Hotel. For one night at least, Charles thought that he had succeeded; he had beaten Thought Control. He had won.

One week later Charles received clear indications that he had been wrong; the experiment was not drawing to an end. November 1 brought the first major snowfall of the year to Burlington: 7.7 inches of snow fell that day, more than the average snowfall for the entire month of November. When Charles walked into Subway that night and shook the snow from his stained and torn coat, Amy approached him sheepishly and told him that he had to leave. Amy's manager had discovered from another employee that he had been stealing bags of potato chips from the display rack by the register. (Amy had pretended not to notice the missing chips because it was so clear that he needed to eat something.) Charles responded with indignation, not to the accusation about the potato chips, but to the demand that he, the owner of Subway, leave his own property.

When Amy warned Charles that she had been instructed to call the police if he refused, he replied, "I would like you to call the police. I would like to have a word with them about this." An officer arrived ten minutes later and issued him a notice of trespass, but Charles did not mention his claims to owning the property. After promising that he would not return, he walked back out into the night, losing his last friend in Burlington and his sanctuary—a place outside of time where the air was warm, the coffee was free, and he was treated with respect; where he communed with his demons, worked on his research, and relived better days.

The arrival of the police carried with it an implicit warning: if Charles was not careful, he would give his persecutors grounds for his arrest and transfer to Vermont State Hospital. Almost ten years after his arrest in Eastman, New Hampshire, the challenge was the same: to stay in control, to not allow himself to become jacked up in response to the experiment or his circumstances. Ten years earlier, the strain had proved too much, and he had become violent. In Burlington, under much worse circumstances, Charles' disorder tricked him into believing that the experiment was about to end. The experiment, of course, continued. Charles was forced to endure the disappointment of seeing his hopes vanish in addition to the continuation of the persecution.

But Charles did not succumb to the pressure. He did not become violent even in the face of what was, from his perspective, extreme provocation. Surrounded by conspirators who pretended not to know what was going on while in fact helping his persecutors goad him into thinking he was crazy, his greatest crime was stealing a bag of potato chips. His self-control and dignity give the lie to the popular image of the schizophrenic as a bloodthirsty, deranged killer. Despite being the victim of profound hardship and irrational thought processes, he did everything in his power to act with restraint. To do otherwise would have resulted in his arrest and the loss of his hard-won freedom. More was at work, however, than mere self-preservation. Charles' restraint owed a lot to his continued faith that people could be made to understand his plight. Both the book of protest that he was writing in his head and his attempts to communicate with those who sat next to him on Church Street were testaments to his optimism about human nature. Implicit in his ongoing effort to find an audience was the belief that if the public could be made to understand the extent of his suffering and the impact on him of their compliance with the wishes of his persecutors, they would help to put an end to the experiment. Despite overwhelming evidence to the contrary, Charles refused to accept the idea that people could be so indifferent to the suffering of another human being.

Chapter 9

The
Thief

Viewed independently of my father's delusions, what was happening to him highlights a major failing in the mental health system, resulting from the same emphasis on civil liberties that contributed to deinstitutionalization: the criminalization of the mentally ill. In many states the legal requirements that have to be met to bring someone to civil court involuntarily for a competency status hearing are so stringent that the mentally ill often wind up being routed through the criminal court system. Once before the court, however, the standards for commitment are the same—usually some variation of the following: the defendant must be shown to be a danger to himself or to others.

This practice affects people with schizophrenia disproportionately because they are less likely to be aware that they are mentally ill, and so are more often in need of involuntary hospitalization. Typically, their condition deteriorates until they wind up living on the street, at which point they are arrested for minor crimes such as panhandling, trespassing, or theft of services. Once before the court, the judge can order a competency status hearing. This roundabout process has distorted statistics of criminality among the mentally ill and contributed to the popular conception of the mentally ill as dangerous. It is also unethical; in effect, it punishes the mentally ill for their symptoms.

The attempts on the part of Charles' persecutors to exploit his insecurities about his mental health by dredging up the past had failed. With the early arrival of winter they switched tactics. Gone were the subtleties of surrogates and the re-creation of elements of his past. Their new strategy could be summed up in three words: *commit or kill.* If they could not get Charles jacked up to the point where he would either break the law or capitulate and accept his diagnosis, they would make sure that he died on the street.

On November 1, 1993, after getting kicked out of Subway, Charles trudged through the snow to the Way Station. He was assigned bed no. 21. His plan was to wait out the winter, using up what was left of his ninety days at the shelter. If he did not realize earlier that he might die on the Marketplace, he realized it the next evening when he arrived at the Way Station to bed down for the night. One hour before he arrived, the director had discovered that Charles' bed was so in-

Howard Bank would cease to exist. He also said that failure to act on the seventeen million dollars would be the Howard Bank's downfall. Then he got up and walked out."

But Charles took Markey's advice. The next morning, after spending another night on a bench, Charles visited the Bank of Vermont at 149 Bank Street and tried to open an account. Unfortunately, his appearance, his demeanor, and his growing reputation on the Marketplace had guaranteed that no area bank would take him as a customer. Almost as soon as he entered the bank, he was intercepted by a security guard and told to leave and not come back. After he left, the bank manager called the police and informed them of the notice of trespass.

Charles returned to the Howard Bank every couple of days to discuss his situation with John Markey. Each time, Markey shook his hand, invited him into his office, and offered him coffee, which Charles accepted. Although Charles seemed to appreciate his hospitality, he continued to make threats against him and the Howard Bank. Markey's background with the FBI had honed his ability to differentiate between serious and innocuous threats. He did not think Charles was dangerous. "I did not get the feeling that he was going to walk back in and do something. It was like he was a palm reader, predicting that we were going to disappear tomorrow, but he was not going to be the cause of it."

Markey did not think Charles was a danger to anyone else; he did believe, however, that he was a danger

fested with lice from the night before that the bedding appeared to be moving of its own accord. He recorded his reaction in the shelter's log: "DO NOT FOR ANY REASON PUT ANYONE IN BEDS 21 & 22 UNTIL I CAN GET THIS PLACE NUKED MANANA. Our friend Chas Lach's bed (21) was *so* infested with body lice that everyone was shocked speechless. I used a whole can of bug spray and cleaned the whole thing with bleach (kills everything), dumped everything in the trash."

After Charles left, the director called the Mobile Crisis Team, a community outreach arm of the Howard Center for Human Services, to tell them that he would no longer be allowed to stay at the Way Station, and to have on record his opinion that Charles was endangering his life through his continued exposure to the elements. He urged Mobile Crisis to perform a psychiatric evaluation of Charles, but he was not optimistic about their recommending his emergency involuntary admission to Vermont State Hospital because Charles was very skilled at controlling the expression of his symptoms whenever his liberty was being threatened. "Whenever a mental health worker would come around to talk to him to try to make an assessment he would all of a sudden become extremely normal, personable, and articulate, which led them to believe that it was his choice to be out here."

Mobile Crisis found Charles that night on a bench on Church Street and interviewed him. Using as their criteria for commitment whether Charles was a danger to himself or others, it was clear that he did not pose a threat to anyone else; it was also clear that he was not suicidal, and, although his feet were found to be frostbitten, the damage was not yet severe enough to be life-threatening.

The next morning at nine o'clock, Charles walked over to the Howard Bank to collect his monthly pension—his temporary reprieve from starvation and the only remaining physical evidence that he had not lived his entire adult life as the transient. He was stunned when he attempted to withdraw a portion of his monthly pension check and was informed by the head teller that his account had been closed as a result of mishandling of funds. Over the previous weeks he had written several NSF (nonsufficient funds) checks to cover the purchase of a winter coat, heavy boots, and meals. He had also accused a teller of stealing money from his account, which no doubt contributed to the bank's decision. Sensitive to Charles' circumstances, the bank had nonetheless accepted that month's wire transfer of his pension. After a brief argument with the bank manager, Charles left with $225 in cash. With his account officially closed, he now had no way to access his SSI benefits, even if his legal guardian managed to locate him and decided to relinquish control over them.

Over the next week—in between countless hours spent alone on the benches on the Marketplace—my father returned again and again to the bank to try to convince someone to reopen his account. With each successive visit his behavior became more bizarre and unpredictable—which brought him to the attention of the head of security at the bank, a former FBI agent named John Markey, whom I met during my visit to Burlington. Middle-aged, with short, cropped silver hair and a confidence born of years of experience dealing with the unexpected, Markey was impressed with the bank's most difficult customer. "You do not forget Charles Lachenmeyer. He was tall. He held himself erect. He was not self-conscious or embarrassed about the way he looked. He had business to do at the bank and he was going to do it. It was obvious to me that he was an intelligent man, a much more intelligent man than myself, but he was *irrational*. He accused the bank of absconding seventeen million dollars that he claimed was owed to him by foreign governments. He also told me that he had seventy-two hundred dollars sitting in a bank in Manchester, New Hampshire, where he had lived for five years before moving to Vermont, and he asked for my help in getting that money transferred to our bank."

Markey told Charles that the Howard Bank would accept the following month's wire transfer of his pension, but that after that he could make no promises. He advised him to open an account at another bank as soon as possible. Charles responded with threats. "He said that by tomorrow I would no longer have a job and th to himself. Watching Charles leave the bank one cold morning after they had shared a pot of coffee, Markey told the bank manager, "That man is going to be found frozen in a snowbank." He was concerned enough about Charles' fate to call the Howard Center for Human Services to try to get him help—an act far removed from his responsibilities as head of security for the bank. The staff at the Howard Center for Human Services confirmed that Charles did, in fact, have $7,200 in funds in New Hampshire that he had not been able to access and told Markey that they were trying to get him involuntarily committed to Vermont State Hospital.

Charles' increased agitation, his wild accusations about specific sums of money, and his grandiose and vague threats all suggested that his condition had begun to deteriorate under the strain of his current circumstances. After months of relative stability, Charles' delusional system was beginning to lose its supportive internal coherence. Until then, he had known that he was impotent and subject to the whims of Thought Control. His challenge had been to maintain his nonviolent protest and his faith in his own sanity. The more powerless he became, however, the more he began to believe that he already had the power and influence he had desired for so long, and thought were his by right— and the more bizarre and unpredictable his behavior became.

At the end of the interview, I shook Markey's hand to convey my appreciation for how he had treated my father. Remembering that he had mentioned that he shook my father's hand each time he saw him, I asked him if he had meant it literally or as a figure of speech. He knew what I was getting at; my father's hands must have been filthy. He told me that he felt it was important to treat him with the same respect he would extend to anyone else, and that he made a point of shaking his hand every time they met. I knew what effect that simple gesture must have had on my father. The transient goes through his days and nights without ever feeling the touch of another human being. After shaking Markey's hand again, I walked out onto the street.

With complaints coming in from so many local institutions—Subway, the Way Station, the Howard Bank, and the Bank of Vermont, among others—the Burlington Police Department began to actively build a case against Charles in an effort to get him off the street. The detective in charge sent a note to the Uniform Services Bureau "requesting that they document all dealings with Lachenmeyer to take proper action towards an Unlawful Trespass charge;" he also contacted John Markey at the Howard Bank and the manager of Subway, requesting that they call the police immediately if Charles returned. Charles' belief that he was the object of an orchestrated conspiracy assisted by Burlington's local population proved to be a self-fulfilling prophecy. The more time passed, the more overlap there was between Charles' delusional world and the actions of the people with whom he came in contact.

At the center of the police department's efforts to build a case against my father was the officer who had kicked him out of Subway at the beginning of November. The only police officer in Burlington permanently assigned to foot patrol, Corporal Robert Booher's beat was the Marketplace. When I met him at the Burlington Police Station, he sported a handlebar mustache, a crew cut, and all the earmarks of being one of the colorful characters indigenous to small cities. I tried to imagine what my father thought of Corporal Booher—who he thought he represented in the experiment—and guessed that he probably saw the most visible police officer on Church Street as a general stand-in for his persecutors and their power.

Corporal Booher's first run-ins with Charles centered on alcohol. When Corporal Booher saw him drinking on Church Street he warned him that the local open container ordinance made it illegal to drink alcohol in a public place. Charles' response surprised Booher. "One thing that really stood out about Charles was—talking with him, I realized very quickly that he was not the normal transient type person as far as intelligence goes. Very articulate, good vocabulary. He used words people do not normally use. One thing that very quickly focused me on his intelligence factor was that he really knew constitutional issues. Police use of force. Our rights. He would talk about Amendment 14, Amendment 3. It was like, okay, I am not going to be able to treat this guy like a normal transient."

Charles was able to catch the police off guard, but he could not prevent them from closing in. His desperate living conditions ensured that he would continue to have trouble with the law. Realizing that he no longer had any hope of receiving his SSI benefits and that access to his pension might be cut off at any moment, Charles was forced to start panhandling on the Marketplace in order to survive. On November 4 at 9 P.M. he stopped two women as they were leaving the Howard Bank ATM and asked them for twenty-five cents. He was seen by a police officer, who, having been briefed about the Trespass Plan, stopped him and issued him an ordinance ticket for panhandling with a citation to appear in court. Charles had the choice of either paying a fifty-dollar fine to the court within seventy-two hours—which he obviously could not afford—or appearing in court on the appointed date for a preliminary hearing to answer charges.

As his situation grew more desperate, Charles depended on legal research in the local library to keep from being arrested—a strategy that drew on his academic training. He knew that if his persecutors could get him in front of a judge, no matter how minor the charge, the judge would be able to order a psychiatric evaluation at Vermont State Hospital. Charles learned quickly from his mistake. Corporal Booher witnessed fested with lice from the night before that the bedding appeared to be moving of its own accord. He recorded his reaction in the shelter's log: "DO NOT FOR ANY REASON PUT ANYONE IN BEDS 21 & 22 UNTIL I CAN GET THIS PLACE NUKED MANANA. Our friend Chas Lach's bed (21) was *so* infested with body lice that everyone was shocked speechless. I used a whole can of bug spray and cleaned the whole thing with bleach (kills everything), dumped everything in the trash."

After Charles left, the director called the Mobile Crisis Team, a community outreach arm of the Howard Center for Human Services, to tell them that he would no longer be allowed to stay at the Way Station, and to have on record his opinion that Charles was endangering his life through his continued exposure to the elements. He urged Mobile Crisis to perform a psychiatric evaluation of Charles, but he was not optimistic about their recommending his emergency involuntary admission to Vermont State Hospital because Charles was very skilled at controlling the expression of his symptoms whenever his liberty was being threatened. "Whenever a mental health worker would come around to talk to him to try to make an assessment he would all of a sudden become extremely normal, personable, and articulate, which led them to believe that it was his choice to be out here."

Mobile Crisis found Charles that night on a bench on Church Street and interviewed him. Using as their criteria for commitment whether Charles was a danger to himself or others, it was clear that he did not pose a threat to anyone else; it was also clear that he was not suicidal, and, although his feet were found to be frost-bitten, the damage was not yet severe enough to be life-threatening.

The next morning at nine o'clock, Charles walked over to the Howard Bank to collect his monthly pension—his temporary reprieve from starvation and the only remaining physical evidence that he had not lived his entire adult life as the transient. He was stunned when he attempted to withdraw a portion of his monthly pension check and was informed by the head teller that his account had been closed as a result of mishandling of funds. Over the previous weeks he had written several NSF (nonsufficient funds) checks to cover the purchase of a winter coat, heavy boots, and meals. He had also accused a teller of stealing money from his account, which no doubt contributed to the bank's decision. Sensitive to Charles' circumstances, the bank had nonetheless accepted that month's wire transfer of his pension. After a brief argument with the bank manager, Charles left with $225 in cash. With his account officially closed, he now had no way to access his SSI benefits, even if his legal guardian managed to locate him and decided to relinquish control over them.

Over the next week—in between countless hours spent alone on the benches on the Marketplace—my father returned again and again to the bank to try to convince someone to reopen his account. With each successive visit his behavior became more bizarre and unpredictable—which brought him to the attention of the head of security at the bank, a former FBI agent named John Markey, whom I met during my visit to Burlington. Middle-aged, with short, cropped silver hair and a confidence born of years of experience dealing with the unexpected, Markey was impressed with the bank's most difficult customer. "You do not forget Charles Lachenmeyer. He was tall. He held himself erect. He was not self-conscious or embarrassed about the way he looked. He had business to do at the bank and he was going to do it. It was obvious to me that he was an intelligent man, a much more intelligent man than myself, but he was *irrational*. He accused the bank of absconding seventeen million dollars that he claimed was owed to him by foreign governments. He also told me that he had seventy-two hundred dollars sitting in a bank in Manchester, New Hampshire, where he had lived for five years before moving to Vermont, and he asked for my help in getting that money transferred to our bank."

Markey told Charles that the Howard Bank would accept the following month's wire transfer of his pension, but that after that he could make no promises. He advised him to open an account at another bank as soon as possible. Charles responded with threats. "He said that by tomorrow I would no longer have a job and the

Howard Bank would cease to exist. He also said that failure to act on the seventeen million dollars would be the Howard Bank's downfall. Then he got up and walked out."

But Charles took Markey's advice. The next morning, after spending another night on a bench, Charles visited the Bank of Vermont at 149 Bank Street and tried to open an account. Unfortunately, his appearance, his demeanor, and his growing reputation on the Marketplace had guaranteed that no area bank would take him as a customer. Almost as soon as he entered the bank, he was intercepted by a security guard and told to leave and not come back. After he left, the bank manager called the police and informed them of the notice of trespass.

Charles returned to the Howard Bank every couple of days to discuss his situation with John Markey. Each time, Markey shook his hand, invited him into his office, and offered him coffee, which Charles accepted. Although Charles seemed to appreciate his hospitality, he continued to make threats against him and the Howard Bank. Markey's background with the FBI had honed his ability to differentiate between serious and innocuous threats. He did not think Charles was dangerous. "I did not get the feeling that he was going to walk back in and do something. It was like he was a palm reader, predicting that we were going to disappear tomorrow, but he was not going to be the cause of it."

Markey did not think Charles was a danger to anyone else; he did believe, however, that he was a danger

to himself. Watching Charles leave the bank one cold morning after they had shared a pot of coffee, Markey told the bank manager, "That man is going to be found frozen in a snowbank." He was concerned enough about Charles' fate to call the Howard Center for Human Services to try to get him help—an act far removed from his responsibilities as head of security for the bank. The staff at the Howard Center for Human Services confirmed that Charles did, in fact, have $7,200 in funds in New Hampshire that he had not been able to access and told Markey that they were trying to get him involuntarily committed to Vermont State Hospital.

Charles' increased agitation, his wild accusations about specific sums of money, and his grandiose and vague threats all suggested that his condition had begun to deteriorate under the strain of his current circumstances. After months of relative stability, Charles' delusional system was beginning to lose its supportive internal coherence. Until then, he had known that he was impotent and subject to the whims of Thought Control. His challenge had been to maintain his nonviolent protest and his faith in his own sanity. The more powerless he became, however, the more he began to believe that he already had the power and influence he had desired for so long, and thought were his by right— and the more bizarre and unpredictable his behavior became.

At the end of the interview, I shook Markey's hand to convey my appreciation for how he had treated my

father. Remembering that he had mentioned that he shook my father's hand each time he saw him, I asked him if he had meant it literally or as a figure of speech. He knew what I was getting at; my father's hands must have been filthy. He told me that he felt it was important to treat him with the same respect he would extend to anyone else, and that he made a point of shaking his hand every time they met. I knew what effect that simple gesture must have had on my father. The transient goes through his days and nights without ever feeling the touch of another human being. After shaking Markey's hand again, I walked out onto the street.

With complaints coming in from so many local institutions—Subway, the Way Station, the Howard Bank, and the Bank of Vermont, among others—the Burlington Police Department began to actively build a case against Charles in an effort to get him off the street. The detective in charge sent a note to the Uniform Services Bureau "requesting that they document all dealings with Lachenmeyer to take proper action towards an Unlawful Trespass charge;" he also contacted John Markey at the Howard Bank and the manager of Subway, requesting that they call the police immediately if Charles returned. Charles' belief that he was the object of an orchestrated conspiracy assisted by Burlington's local population proved to be a self-fulfilling prophecy. The more time passed, the more over-

lap there was between Charles' delusional world and the actions of the people with whom he came in contact.

At the center of the police department's efforts to build a case against my father was the officer who had kicked him out of Subway at the beginning of November. The only police officer in Burlington permanently assigned to foot patrol, Corporal Robert Booher's beat was the Marketplace. When I met him at the Burlington Police Station, he sported a handlebar mustache, a crew cut, and all the earmarks of being one of the colorful characters indigenous to small cities. I tried to imagine what my father thought of Corporal Booher—who he thought he represented in the experiment—and guessed that he probably saw the most visible police officer on Church Street as a general stand-in for his persecutors and their power.

Corporal Booher's first run-ins with Charles centered on alcohol. When Corporal Booher saw him drinking on Church Street he warned him that the local open container ordinance made it illegal to drink alcohol in a public place. Charles' response surprised Booher. "One thing that really stood out about Charles was—talking with him, I realized very quickly that he was not the normal transient type person as far as intelligence goes. Very articulate, good vocabulary. He used words people do not normally use. One thing that very quickly focused me on his intelligence factor was that he really knew constitutional issues. Police use of force. Our

rights. He would talk about Amendment 14, Amendment 3. It was like, okay, I am not going to be able to treat this guy like a normal transient."

Charles was able to catch the police off guard, but he could not prevent them from closing in. His desperate living conditions ensured that he would continue to have trouble with the law. Realizing that he no longer had any hope of receiving his SSI benefits and that access to his pension might be cut off at any moment, Charles was forced to start panhandling on the Marketplace in order to survive. On November 4 at 9 P.M. he stopped two women as they were leaving the Howard Bank ATM and asked them for twenty-five cents. He was seen by a police officer, who, having been briefed about the Trespass Plan, stopped him and issued him an ordinance ticket for panhandling with a citation to appear in court. Charles had the choice of either paying a fifty-dollar fine to the court within seventy-two hours—which he obviously could not afford—or appearing in court on the appointed date for a preliminary hearing to answer charges.

As his situation grew more desperate, Charles depended on legal research in the local library to keep from being arrested—a strategy that drew on his academic training. He knew that if his persecutors could get him in front of a judge, no matter how minor the charge, the judge would be able to order a psychiatric evaluation at Vermont State Hospital. Charles learned quickly from his mistake. Corporal Booher witnessed

firsthand how his panhandling technique evolved. "Our city ordinance is very clear: you have to ask people directly for money. Charles must have found that out because all of a sudden he started to ask people, 'Can you help me out?' I actually brought this to the city attorney's attention and she was under the impression that it would not hold water in court. He found a way to beat the system. That was unique among the transients."

Charles' victory was short-lived. As November gave way to December, the drop in temperature and increased snowfall reduced pedestrian traffic on the Marketplace to a minimum, thwarting Charles' efforts to panhandle. For hours at a time Charles was the only person Corporal Booher would see while on patrol—a dark, solitary figure silhouetted against falling snow. "That was a hard winter and I would see him standing on a corner in a thin khaki jacket with his hands in his pockets. Sometimes, he didn't even put his hands in his pockets. And we are talking when the temperature was *twenty below!* He would be out when *no one* was out, and he would stand there for *hours*. I was amazed that we did not find him glued to a park bench."

By this time, even other transients began to avoid Charles; he was too agitated and delusional to talk to even in passing. He spent his days entirely alone, sitting on benches, walking up and down the Marketplace, ducking into a diner to get out of the cold whenever he panhandled enough change for a cup of coffee; the nights he endured outside, sleeping fitfully on a park bench or pacing up and down Church Street to keep warm. After using up all of December's pension money he resorted to living entirely off of whatever he was still able to panhandle from passersby.

On December 17, Charles failed to appear at his preliminary hearing for the November 4 panhandling charge. The judge ordered a warrant for his arrest. Ten days later, on December 27, the day the warrant was issued, a monthlong record-breaking cold stretch began. The high that day was five degrees and the low, *without wind chill*, was seventeen below zero. Somehow he survived the month. On the morning of December 29, Corporal Booher arrested him at the intersection of Church and College streets and transported him to the Chittenden County Court.

The Chittenden County Court does not employ stenographers; hearings are recorded on audiotape. While in Burlington, I visited the courthouse and made copies of my father's December 29 preliminary hearing and the hearings that followed. His voice sounded exactly the way it did in my memory. It was strange to try to impose on that strong, clear voice the image of an unkempt, lice-infested transient, not just because in my mind's eye my father is always thirty-five, handsome, and strong; at the hearing his manner of speech had a precision, a confidence, and a directness that belied his circumstances. The only "flaw" in his voice was a slightly clipped delivery, as if he had to really work to stay calm, which I am sure was the case. Under extremely stressful conditions, he had to be careful not to exhibit any behavior that would call into question his mental health. He pleaded not guilty to the charge of panhandling. At the end of the hearing the judge released him on his own recognizance and set the calendar call for January 21 at 2:30 P.M. The recording of the proceedings makes it clear that despite his circumstances, my father had not lost his wit or his appreciation of irony:

JUDGE: Okay, Mr. Lachenmeyer, the court officer's going to give you a piece of paper which has the date of your next appearance to be here for the calendar call.

LACHENMEYER: Sure. Would you know what that date is?

COURT OFFICER: January twenty-first.

JUDGE: January twenty-first of 1994. It's a Friday.

LACHENMEYER: January twenty-first?

JUDGE: Yes, yes.

LACHENMEYER: What is today?

JUDGE: Today is December twenty-ninth.

LACHENMEYER: Oh, sure, that's good. That's good.

The sarcasm was apparent in Charles' voice. To a transient the calendar loses all meaning; one day is the same as another.

JUDGE: Okay, so it's there on that piece of paper. So if you just hang on to that as a reminder of when to be here next . . .

STATE: And Mr. Lachenmeyer understands his obligation to appear?

LACHENMEYER: Excuse me?

STATE: You understand your obligation to appear at that time?

LACHENMEYER: Sure. I'll be here in a three-piece suit with the Queen of England.

Charles knew that the court was not going to dismiss the case or put him in jail for a few days as punishment in lieu of paying the fifty-dollar fine. The next phase in their machinations would be a competency status hearing, resulting in his being committed to Vermont State Hospital. In three weeks he would be returned to the role of prisoner; his escape from Manchester and his nine months of suffering on the streets of Burlington were going to be for nothing. The only way out was to flee Burlington as soon as his pension check arrived at the Howard Bank on January 1. But Charles knew that his check was not going to arrive.

At four o'clock in the afternoon on New Year's Eve Corporal Booher responded to a disorderly conduct complaint at the Bank of Vermont. While employees were setting up chairs inside the bank for a concert scheduled as part of the Burlington First Night Festival, customers using the ATM in the lobby reported that a transient had walked in and shouted repeatedly, "I want slaughter and death here!" The transient was gone by the time Corporal Booher arrived on the scene, but he knew from the description that it was Charles.

Charles reemerged from wherever he was hiding after dark. At nine o'clock that evening Corporal Booher found him sitting quietly on a bench in City Hall Park and asked him what happened. "He denied the incident at the bank as described by the employee. He told me that he was having problems with both the Bank of Vermont and the Howard Bank; that he had been in the process of switching accounts from one bank to the other when 'they' lost his money. This was his reason for his aggression toward the banking business."

Charles, anticipating that the Howard Bank would refuse his next direct deposit, had given the company that distributed his pension the Bank of Vermont address in the hope that he might be able to convince them in the interim to open an account for him. But his gambit had failed; his monthly pension check did not arrive at either the Howard Bank or the Bank of Vermont. Without a home address or telephone number or access to funds, and burdened by his symptoms, Charles had no hope of rectifying the situation on his own.

He was trapped. Without his pension he had no way of leaving Burlington before the twenty-first of January. More important, he had no way to feed himself

or even buy a cup of coffee to allow him a respite, however brief, from what was shaping up to be one of the
harshest winters in Burlington's history.

After warning Charles to stop threatening people and
to stay away from the Bank of Vermont, Corporal Booher
left him alone in the park. Three hours later, at midnight, when the eruption of muffled cheers and car
horns heralded the arrival of 1994, the temperature
dropped to five below zero, and the worst year in
Charles' life ended the way it had begun—with the
promise of more hardship to come and no relief in
sight.

In January the temperature in Burlington dropped to
a historic low: an average high for the month of
seventeen degrees and an average low of three below
zero without wind chill factor. The cumulative snowfall that month was more than twice the average for
January: 38.6 inches. On the fourth alone, almost ten
inches of snow fell on downtown Burlington. Charles
had only one place where he could escape from
the relentless cold—in just over one year he had gone
from opening an account at the Howard Bank to sleeping in its ATM. It is unclear what and where Charles
ate during the first two weeks of the new year. What
is clear is that he lost a lot of weight. During that
time he also developed a severe limp and was
coughing almost continually. From his perspective,

his persecutors' plan had indeed become—commit or kill.

Early on the morning of January 12, Charles woke up in the ATM and stepped out onto the Marketplace. He was wearing a green army jacket over a brown sweater and soiled blue slacks. His head and hands were bare. It was eight degrees outside. Charles could not ignore his hunger any longer. He walked west along Bank Street until he came to Henry's Diner, a traditional American diner with a red neon sign over the door, where he had been a regular customer the previous winter. He sat at a booth by the window and ordered three scrambled eggs with corned beef hash and coffee, and followed it with a second breakfast of pancakes and sausages, topped off by two slices of apple pie. After he had finished eating, he spent the rest of the morning looking out the window, watching customers come and go, and drinking free refills of coffee.

At the end of three hours, a customer finally complained about how badly Charles smelled. The owner, emboldened by the burgeoning lunch crowd and the drain on income his presence represented, asked him to pay up and leave. Charles took the request in stride, replying that he would leave as soon as he finished his cup of coffee. When he did leave, he skipped out on the bill, which totaled $10.07. On the brink of starvation, Charles had, for the second time in his life—the first being the potato chips—stolen something from someone else. The owner called the police and reported the theft of services. Corporal Booher canvassed the Marketplace looking for Charles, but was unable to locate him.

The next morning Charles walked along Bank Street in the opposite direction and ate another huge meal at the aptly named Oasis Diner, then told the waiter with a smile that he did not have any money. This time Charles waited calmly for the police to arrive. He was picked up, issued a citation for theft of services, and released. Later that morning, a police officer who had been alerted about the previous day's theft of services at Henry's Diner arrested Charles outside the Howard Bank ATM and brought him to the Burlington police station, where he was issued another citation, and again released.

When the officer asked my father before arresting him if he had committed the theft of services, he said, "I ate breakfast there, but they're wrong. My son paid the tab." When I read those words in the police report for the first time, my thinking temporarily crossed over into the irrational. I felt as though my father had intentionally left a message for me embedded in his police record—as if he knew that I would, after his death, try to learn about this part of his life. I was convinced that his message was—don't kid yourself; no matter what you try to do, you will never absolve yourself of the sin of having abandoned me.

Although there is no way to know for certain, it *is*

conceivable that my father may have been trying to send me a message when he made that statement to the police. If he really did believe that I was now a willing participant in the experiment, it would follow that I was aware of his circumstances in Burlington and that his comment might, in fact, be passed on to me. The idea that my father may have believed that I turned my back on him with full knowledge of the extent of his suffering is the most horrible thought I can imagine. I can only hope that he himself was not capable of imagining that the son he had raised was capable of such indifference.

After being arrested outside the Howard Bank ATM for the theft of services at Henry's Diner, Charles stopped sleeping there at night. With nowhere else to go, he sought shelter in any doorway he could gain access to on the Marketplace. Complaint after complaint was called in to the police by proprietors and residents over the next few days as Charles moved from doorway to doorway in an effort to stay out of the cold. A half dozen area restaurants also called to report thefts of services involving Charles. On January 17 another 5.6 inches of snow fell on Burlington. The temperature continued to plummet. On January 18 the low for the day was minus twenty degrees, *minus fifty degrees* with wind chill. At 6:30 A.M. that morning the director of the Way Station wrote in the daily log that "the Police were across the street rousting Charles Lachenmeyer out of the 84 Church Street entryway. I went across and spoke with them and explained what was going on. They are anxiously awaiting a bench warrant to be issued so they can have him evaluated medically. Until then they cannot do much because he goes into his polite and lucid mode when they question him." The calendar call on the panhandling charge was still three days away.

At midnight on January 18 Charles returned to the Way Station to try to get in out of the cold. The extent of his recent psychological deterioration was apparent. The director described their interaction in the log. "Charles Lachenmeyer odyssey continues: Charles came in and started to walk through the dorm. I called him back out into the lobby. He insisted that he 'had a right to come in here.' He was agitated and angry and started to shout. He said, 'I am the Commander-in-Chief!' Then he waved his hand at me and said, 'Poof! You are gone. Poof! The police are gone. Poof! Everybody is gone.' I called the police. They ran Charles off."

Charles' delusional system had evidently unraveled completely. His ten-year-long fixation on Thought Control had come to an end. His claims, accusations, and threats no longer had any obvious internal coherence. There was still, however, emotional coherence. The more disenfranchised, confused, and isolated Charles became, the more powerful he became in his delusional world. He had apparently even begun to believe that he was the President of the United States. If he did, it would not have done much to alleviate his physical or psychological suffering; no delusion of potency could override his experience of homelessness or the symptoms of schizophrenia.

Over the next three days phone calls about Charles fired back and forth between the Way Station, Mobile Crisis, and the Burlington Police Department. Everyone was waiting anxiously for his court date on January 21, afraid that he might die before then from exposure. Charles in the meantime kept a low profile; no trespass or theft of services citations were issued. No one knew where he slept or what he ate. Unless he was finding scraps of food in garbage cans, he was not eating at all. On the twenty-first, as expected, Charles failed to appear in court. The judge again ordered a warrant for his arrest.

On the evening of the twenty-fifth, Charles was still at large. Late that night he called up his past from a pay phone on the Marketplace. After having been out of touch for almost thirty years, he called his former roommate at the College of William and Mary, Brian Chabot—a conversation Chabot characterized as the most frightening of his life. "Charles said that he had been involved in some drug smuggling out of Cuba, and that the CIA was coming after him. He accused me of leading the authorities to him. I told him that I didn't know anything about it, but he refused to believe me. He was a totally different person from the person I knew in college, but he was still a very articulate and vivid man, and he painted a picture that could have been true. I had no reason not to believe that it was real at some level.

"The phone call went on for a long time, maybe an hour. Every few minutes he dropped change into the pay phone. Eventually, I was able to convince him that I had no knowledge of his life or what he was up to. After that, we reminisced a little about the old days, but it did not last for long. At the end of the call I wished him well and asked him to take care of himself. I remember crying when I put the phone down. It was such an emotional interaction, both out of a sense of fear, and then a sense of fear for him, for his future. Before he hung up he told me that he was escaping to Canada to stay ahead of the law. He said that he had a dog with him—he said that he had no other friend in the world except the dog—and that he was heading off to Canada. That was the first time I had heard from him since college and I never heard from him again."

My father had not owned a dog in ten years, not since the police took Georgie away when he was first committed to New Hampshire Hospital. In fact, his statement may have been a reference to that time, the last time he was jacked up to the point of being violent. If the dog is removed from the equation—as, indeed, it was—his statement becomes, simply, "I do not have a friend in the world."

In 1989, Clifford took photographs of my father during his visit to New York for Joel's wedding—the occasion he had suggested for our father-son reunion. In one picture my father is sitting on a couch petting a gray-muzzled Labrador. Just enough of his face is showing to reveal that he is smiling. Despite his circumstances, my father was happy at the moment the picture was taken. The reason is obvious: a dog does not judge a man by where he is in life or how far removed he is from his goals and past accomplishments; nor does he judge the quality or content of his thoughts or speech. A dog responds to whatever is good in a man. There was still good in my father in 1989; and there was still good in him during the winter of 1993—there was still the possibility of happiness—but there was no one left to draw it out of him. My father's call to Chabot was probably made in the hope that his former friend would offer him assistance. His pride and his symptoms, however, combined to prevent him from being direct, just as they had in his last letter to me, in his letter to Dr. Burchard, and in his last phone call to his cousin, Marilyn.

The day after the phone call to Brian Chabot, Corporal Booher found Charles at the local library, walking through the stacks, inspecting its meager collection of sociology books. Corporal Booher arrested him and brought him to the courthouse, where his

erratic behavior led the presiding judge to schedule a
competency status hearing and order that he be sent in
the interim to Vermont State Hospital in Waterbury for
a psychiatric evaluation. Charles' time on the street had
finally come to an end.

Sitting with me in the Burlington police station three
years later, Corporal Booher handed me my father's
wallet, which had been sitting in his file, forgotten,
since his death. I looked through it quickly, working
hard to hold back any display of emotion. I found the
card from the Howard Center for Human Services that
the police officer had used in his effort to locate the
next of kin. My father's case manager had written
down on the card that this next appointment was scheduled for January 17, 1995. There were several receipts
for photocopies made at Kinko's in the billfold and a
single dollar bill. In the change purse was eighty-seven
cents.

When I returned to my hotel I examined the wallet
more closely, hoping, irrationally under the circumstances, to find a photograph of my father and me—
evidence that he had not forgotten me. There was nothing. I threw away his receipts and the card from the
Howard Center and arranged the $1.87 in a small pile
on the bed. I could not bring myself to set the money
aside and give it special meaning. I also could not bring
myself to put it in my wallet and return it to circula-

tion. I was offended by its indifference to the fate of my father. It bothered me that if I spent it, the following week it would be used to buy an upscale coffee or a few packs of gum. I kept thinking to myself that the year before he died my father literally did not have a dollar to his name and had had to steal in order to eat. In the end, I threw the coins in the garbage, after hiding them in a wad of wet toilet paper so they would not be discovered when the trash was emptied. Then I tore the bill up into tiny pieces and flushed it down the toilet. The absurdity of my impromptu ritual made me feel a little better, giving me the strength to look at the other thing Corporal Booher had given me from my father's file.

I sat back down on the bed and stared at a Polaroid photograph of my father. Taken in the Burlington police station after his arrest, it was the difference between being told that someone had died and seeing the corpse in the casket at the funeral home. I had grown used to hearing the description of my father as a transient in Burlington . . . long hair, beard, unkempt. Seeing him undid the familiarity of the words. The photograph itself was a sad but unremarkable image of a too-thin man with an overgrown beard, a receding hairline, and eyes that stared unblinking at the world. For it to mean anything special you had to have heard the voice, smelled the skin, felt the stubble on his cheeks, the strength in his hug, the confidence and love of a father for his only son. There was no way to get from that memory to the image I held in my hand. All the traveling, all the conversations, all the explanations, all the words could not bridge those two worlds.

That night before I fell asleep, I imagined superimposed upon the dark walls of my hotel room in one giant collage the thousands upon thousands of photographs that I knew must be buried in files in police stations across the country: transients who had been arrested for petty crimes like trespassing, panhandling, and theft of services; abandoned photographs of abandoned lives. I found myself thinking of the day in Times Square in 1978 when I saw the transient for the first time. Suddenly I had a fanciful revelation: I knew what the transient had tried to say to my father and me as we walked past him. It came to me with the force of fact—he was trying to warn us.

Chapter 10

The
Patient

Located in Waterbury, home to the corporate headquarters of Ben & Jerry's Ice Cream and Green Mountain Coffee, Vermont State Hospital's patient population had dropped from a high of sixteen hundred patients in 1955 to fifty when I visited in 1997. There had been rumors for years that it would close. Of the remaining patients, most were diagnosed with schizophrenia. Vermont State Hospital was my first introduction to life on a closed ward at a state hospital. I drifted through halls lined with people marching to their own drum. It was obvious from how they reacted to my presence that they did not have many visitors: one elderly man came up to me over and over again to shake my hand; another man— middle-aged and obese—gave me the thumbs up, then retreated into his room; a petite woman scowled at me from an oversized vinyl chair. Very few of the patients at the hospital in 1997 were there in 1994. Those who remained remembered my father as a remote figure who kept to himself.

On January 26, 1994, almost ten years after his first admission to New Hampshire Hospital, Charles became Patient 26845 at Vermont State Hospital. His progress notes indicated that the day he arrived he requested extra food after both lunch and dinner because he was still hungry. That evening he agreed to take a bath as part of the delousing process—his first bath or shower since living on the streets. His clothes were deloused, cleaned, and returned to him. Charles appeared to be no more cowed by his sudden loss of freedom than he had been by the loss of his apartment eleven months earlier. On the ward, he kept to himself and refused all offers of treatment. He was kept under observation until February 1, when a court-appointed psychiatrist examined him in preparation for the competency hearing to follow.

According to the psychiatrist's evaluative report, Charles managed to retain his composure during the interview, despite the fact that he was being detained against his will and that his mental health was again being challenged. His delusions were, however, very much in evidence and had, if anything, become more bizarre. The psychiatrist recorded in his notes, "Mr. Lachenmeyer was extremely delusional, stating that he was the Commander-in-Chief of the United States Armed Forces. He said that there was no state of Vermont; that the whole country was just one unit, Federally-controlled, and that he was in charge. He indicated that he had been 'preprogrammed' and 'trained to be like this.' He stated that he had 27 zillion dollars in the bank. He said that he 'hunts he who offends.' When I asked him to elaborate on this, he said that he might give orders for someone to be shot or hung, but that he was not a violent man and denied any significant history of violence. He also went on to say that there was no such thing as violence. He stated that President Reagan had personally ordered his prior 1984 hospitalization in New Hampshire, but he denied feeling that he was the object of any evil schemes at this time. He is not currently suicidal, but he said he was once, a long time ago."

Like John Markey, the head of security at Howard Bank, the psychiatrist concluded that Charles was not dangerous; it was clear that there was no risk he would carry out his threats. "He pointed up toward the heavens and informed me that the police officers who had arrested him were no longer on the force; that they had given up their badges and guns and had gone on high. He then meandered on into a disjointed statement about mountaineering. He appeared to be suffering from the delusion that he could at any time obliterate the society in which he lived, including the Chittenden County Court, the hospital in which he was presently held, and the hospital in New Hampshire, simply by giving voice to his desire."

Late in the interview, Charles made explicit what his claims of omniscience and his use of Biblical language and phrasing implied. "He requested that he be allowed to communicate with God. I told him, 'Go ahead.' He looked up and started to talk to God. I did not see God, but he did apparently." An ardent Atheist his whole adult life, Charles was now, under the influence of schizophrenia, not only an ardent believer, but a self-proclaimed prophet with direct access to God. It was impossible to know whether or not the religious turn his delusions had taken had anything to do with him hearing his mother's voice or her early efforts to convert him to Christian Science.

As shocked as I was to read the evidence of my father's increasingly bizarre thought processes, I was just as surprised by the clarity and wit with which he expressed his conviction that he was sane. Near the end of his evaluation, the psychiatrist reported, "When I asked Charles if he thought he had a mental illness, he said that he did and that his mental illness was, 'love of life and humanity.'" My father's progressive deterioration had apparently not compromised his intelligence. It *is* crazy to love life and humanity when life and humanity have conspired to strip you of everything, even the sanctity of your mind and sense of self. My father's ironic response to the psychiatrist's question demonstrated that he was himself aware that his determination to not get jacked up and to continue to work on his book of protest, even after his transformation into the transient, was a resilient expression of faith and hope. He had not given up on the world that had given up on him.

Despite Charles' stubborn insistence that he was sane, the psychiatrist concluded in his evaluation that chronic paranoid schizophrenia with acute exacerbation "would seem to best account for Charles' severe social decline and lack of any social network" and for the fact that "most of his conversation was delusional and unfocused, suggestive of a profound thought disorder." Although of the opinion that Charles did not represent a danger to others, the psychiatrist was convinced that he would be "a danger to himself should he be released into the community from his present hospitalization. He is severely malnourished and underweight, and has already suffered frostbite. With the present subzero temperatures, his chances of surviving on the street are minimal." The psychiatrist recommended in his evaluation that Charles be officially committed to Vermont State Hospital. With reference to the panhandling charge brought against him by the state, ostensibly the reason he was initially brought before the court, the psychiatrist concluded, "When I examined him he was not competent to stand trial. There is support for a plea of not guilty by reason of insanity."

My father's competency status hearing on the panhandling charge was scheduled for March 18, 1994, but in mid-February he was transported back to Chittenden County Court for a preliminary hearing on the theft of services charges at Henry's Diner and the Oasis Diner. I was shocked when I played the audio recording of this hearing and heard the change in my father's voice. Gone was the strong, clear voice I had known growing up and which had still been evident at his December 29 hearing. What the cassette tape recorded was my father parodying a heavy Brooklyn accent.

JUDGE: Good afternoon, Mr. Lachenmeyer.

LACHENMEYER: How'ya doin'?

JUDGE: Pretty well, thank you. Have you gotten copies of the State's new complaints against you?

LACHENMEYER: Which state?

JUDGE: Hmm?

LACHENMEYER: Which state?

JUDGE: The State of Vermont's complaint against you.

LACHENMEYER: No, I ain't. I'm indigent. Nobody gave me a copy of nothin'. Somebody sign this? Good luck.

JUDGE: Here we go. You do not have them because I do. I will read them out loud to you, all right? The State charges that on January twelfth—

LACHENMEYER: They're lyin' sons of bitches! Oh, apology.

JUDGE: The State charges that on January twelfth, 1994, you were a person who obtained services by deception which you knew to be available only for pay, that is, a meal at Henry's Diner—

LACHENMEYER: Um-hmm.

JUDGE: —valued at ten dollars and that on January thirteenth you did the same thing at the Oasis Diner for $10.54. This is an arraignment for you to

make a formal response to the State's complaint
against you. Is the State seeking more than a fine
here?

STATE'S ATTORNEY: Yes, Your Honor, there is a restitution
issue.

LACHENMEYER: Res, res, what's restitute?

JUDGE: Would you like a public defender to help you out?

At this point, Charles revealed to the court that he
had been playing a game: his accent was fake, the allu-
sion to Brooklyn possibly a roundabout way of telling
his persecutors that he was aware that they were trying
to get him to think he possessed his mother's demons.
Realizing that he had pushed the I'm-an-indigent-
from-Brooklyn-routine too far, to a point where his only
remaining source of credibility, his intelligence, was
being dismissed, he switched tactics. Suddenly, all trace
of Brooklyn was gone from his speech and he sounded
like himself again.

LACHENMEYER: No. What is the nature of this hearing? Do
you want me to plead guilty or innocent?

JUDGE: Yeah.

LACHENMEYER: Innocent. Innocent as hell and everybody
in here knows it.

JUDGE: All right. That makes it simple. Do you want a
lawyer to help you out?

LACHENMEYER: The whole court system is a mockery. A
total mockery.

JUDGE: Do you want a lawyer to help you out, sir?

LACHENMEYER: No. Help me out of what?

JUDGE: All right, the Court is going to—

LACHENMEYER: The whole system is based on God and Natural Law and, of course, you are making a mockery of God and Natural Law.

A police siren can be heard passing close by the courthouse.

LACHENMEYER: Uh-oh. Somebody is hurt.

JUDGE: We better order an outpatient—an inpatient evaluation of Mr. Lachenmeyer on competency and sanity.

LACHENMEYER: He loves women, saves babies from death, resurrects the dead, makes people rich. Why not.

From there, the proceedings devolved into farce, succumbing to the distraction of Charles' non sequiturs. The judge made a second attempt to order that Charles be sent for an inpatient evaluation at Vermont State Hospital, only to be reminded by the state's attorney that Charles had just come from there and that there was a competency status hearing scheduled the following month with regard to the earlier panhandling charge. It was at this point that Charles made explicit what his Brooklyn accent had hinted at earlier in the hearing.

LACHENMEYER: Yeah. I have got to go back. I miss my mother. She is at the state hospital.

Ignoring Charles' statement, the judge brought the proceeding to a close as quickly as possible, and Charles was taken by the sheriff's department back to Vermont State Hospital to await his competency status hearing.

When I sat down in the day hall with Dr. Richard Munson, my father's psychiatrist at Vermont State Hospital, I liked him from the start. He was soft-spoken and learned—his speech was peppered with literary and philosophical allusions—and he clearly cared about his patients, past and present. As we talked, an audience gathered slowly; patients drifted into the room and sat down in chairs near us, pretending to watch television, but obviously curious about any break in the daily routine on the ward.

Dr. Munson's recollection of an interview with Charles that took place on the ward prior to his competency hearing suggested that the recent shifts in his delusional system had remained intact. "His speech was rapid and almost nonstop. He told me that just before I walked over he had received a message from God to speak openly to me. He claimed that he was in constant communication with God and government agencies, and he believed that I received this information as well. He said I had communicated my thoughts to him in the day hall while sitting in my office. In order to transmit a message to me when I was not in the same room, all he had to do was speak aloud. He said that he was Commander-in-Chief and the King of England. He said he would be released soon and we would all be arrested and shot. When I asked if he intended to shoot people, he said, 'I am licensed to kill. I am MI-5. I have a Beretta, but that will be obviated by what will happen to you.' "

Despite the increased grandiosity and incoherence of his delusional claims over the prior few months, Charles quickly settled into a daily routine at Vermont State Hospital that was almost identical to his routine at New Hampshire Hospital ten years earlier. He again positioned himself as the outsider on the ward, spatially and socially. Dr. Munson recalled, "Whenever possible, Charles avoided contact with staff and patients. He would observe everything that was happening around him, but never participated in any social activities. He spent most of his time sitting alone in one particular chair in the day hall, writing in a notebook. He would never show anyone what he was working on. He mumbled to himself a lot and continually refused the offer of medication, insisting that he was not ill." It is impossible to know for certain what he was writing. If the past is any indication, it is likely that he was continuing his protest against the conspiracy; he may even have been putting down on paper the book he reported writing in his head while living on the street. But there is no way to predict what impact his new delusions might have had on his perspective.

During this period, only one subject seemed to goad

Charles into interacting with the staff and patients: cigarettes. Almost all of his progress notes over the next month centered on the issue of smoking—recalling the notes in his 1964 journal on the importance of smoking to patients at Eastern State Hospital. On the street, Charles had become accustomed to smoking cigarettes whenever and wherever he could bum them off of passersby. On the ward, patients were only allowed to smoke during scheduled smoking breaks, and were restricted to a small screened-in porch that looked out on the grounds of the hospital. Charles threatened on several occasions to use force to get on the smoking porch in between designated smoking breaks, and, although he never made good on his threats, on several occasions he became agitated enough for the staff to escort him to the solitary room.

Charles' frustration with the smoking issue was exacerbated by the fact that unlike most of the other patients on the ward, who were receiving SSI benefits, he had no source of income with which to purchase cigarettes. The staff was unaware of the existence of his pension. They had discovered that he was entitled to receive SSI benefits and that these benefits were still controlled by his legal guardian in New Hampshire, who had lost touch with Charles after he became homeless. It was not until March 10, after Charles had been institutionalized for six weeks, that arrangements were finalized with the legal guardian for him to receive one hundred fifty dollars a month for spending money and cigarettes. In the interim, Charles was obliged to continue practices he had had to resort to on the Marketplace; namely, begging. His progress notes documented his success: "There is some question if he intimidates patients either by his size and appearance or by what he says. In any case, it is effective and he always seems to have a cigarette."

After listening to the audio recording of my father's March 18 competency status hearing, I was eager to talk with someone who had witnessed the proceeding firsthand. When the presiding judge, Marilyn Skoaglund, agreed to meet me at the Chittenden County Court, she confirmed that what had transpired that day was unusual. Although she had presided over thousands of cases since then, most involving more memorable crimes than panhandling, she remembered it well. "Mr. Lachenmeyer was a very impressive, intense, handsome man. Long hair, beard, strong personality. A real presence. There are times when a defendant in court rarely meets your eyes, will not look at you. They are very beaten down and defeated by life when they come into this process. Mr. Lachenmeyer was none of those. I mean, immediately he stood out from the average defendant coming in here *without* a mental illness facing a charge. This was *his* hearing and he felt quite free to comment on what was going on."

The audiotape of the hearing revealed Charles'

active involvement in the proceedings. When the state's attorney called the court-appointed psychiatrist to the stand—the same psychiatrist who had performed his psychiatric evaluation at Vermont State Hospital— Charles leaned into his microphone and stated in an authoritative voice, "I object. He is incompetent." From that point on, he punctuated the proceedings with his objections, despite his public defender's admonishments for him to be quiet. For Charles, this hearing was the distillation of his entire struggle since arriving in Vermont. After enduring a year of enforced homelessness, technological transformations, surrogates, and all manner of coercion, everything was finally out in the open. His persecutors were about to label him insane again and deprive him of his freedom despite his having kept himself from getting jacked up. From his point of view, the only thing he was guilty of was his determination to survive the indignities and suffering they had imposed upon him.

Judge Skoaglund could not know the role that Charles' delusional system had assigned to her; she was taken very much by surprise by what happened next. "It was clear that everyone was in agreement that Mr. Lachenmeyer needed hospitalization and was suffering from schizophrenia. After the witness got down from the stand and I started to deliver my ruling from the bench, Mr. Lachenmeyer interrupted, asking in a very strong, authoritative voice, 'Do I have the right to make a statement? Can I make a statement?' I hesitated, then

I told him yes, but asked him to be brief. What happened next had never before happened to me with a defendant and has never happened since. Mr. Lachenmeyer pronounced sentence on *me* before I could pronounce sentence on *him!*"

His voice was strong, clear, and commanding; he was submitting a statement of fact, delivered without emotion and with complete conviction: "You are not here. None of you have any credentials to be here. I am President of the United States, Commander-in-Chief of the United States Armed Forces. You all know that fact. You are in violation of all military known statutes. You are hereby subject to the penalty of hanging and firing squad. Everything in here is a lie and joke. And *that* is reality. I have made my statement. Do you want me to sign it? *Charles W. Lachenmeyer, Ph.D.*"

In pronouncing sentence on the judge, the attorneys, and the state's witness, Charles was attempting to impose his interpretation of reality on the people who had insisted on imposing their interpretation of reality on him for more than a decade. Living in a society that had tried again and again to convince him that he was mentally ill—a society in which having a mental illness is often synonymous with a life of suffering, prejudice, and abandonment—he wanted to have in the public record his insistence on his self-worth as a person and his belief that he was still someone. He was not just a transient, a petty criminal, a problem; he was a man who had accomplished and who had fulfilled all the expectations a society has of its members. He had studied. He had worked hard. He had taught. He had raised a son. He had struggled to belong. He had struggled to survive. Charles never forgot what he had accomplished before his life fell apart. He never forgot that he was and always would be *Charles W. Lachenmeyer, Ph.D.*

In our lives, we each face moments that test our convictions and our character, and it is these moments that define us—not what we do before, not what we do after. Whatever I accomplish in my life will never equal what my father accomplished as a mentally ill transient in the Chittenden County Court in Burlington, Vermont, in 1994. Most of us are so used to defining ourselves and our self-worth in relation to our possessions and the perceptions of others that we would not have the necessary strength to insist that we still are who we once were if we found ourselves stripped of everything and everyone in our lives.

Starting in 1990 a new generation of antipsychotic medications began to lead to significant improvements in the treatment of people with schizophrenia. Often referred to as atypical antipsychotic medications, they have been shown to be more effective than older antipsychotic medications such as Haloperidol in reducing symptoms, and for the most part have fewer side effects. To date, atypical antipsychotic medications are available only in pill form, however, which limits their utility for the roughly 40 percent of people with schizophrenia who do not recognize that they are ill, and are, therefore, likely not to comply with treatment. For this reason, when the court finally authorized involuntary medication for Charles that September, Dr. Munson put him back on a monthly injection of Haloperidol.

Charles' condition improved quickly. He stopped pacing the halls and making threatening gestures. His speech became more logical and spontaneous. He began to interact more often and more successfully with the staff and other patients. Charles, for example, found an informed and interested listener in Dr. Munson, with whom he discussed classic works of sociology and psychology as well as his own research. Dr. Munson was impressed. "I did not feel like we were psychiatrist and patient. I looked on Charles as an equal and tried to treat him as one. He was incredibly bright, very quick. Most of the time he was way ahead of me, but then the delusions would resurface and derail the conversation."

Initially, even with the benefit of medication, Charles' symptoms did not diminish to the point where Dr. Munson felt he was ready for a conditional discharge. In late September he described in Charles' progress notes a meeting they had had to discuss his treatment and aftercare plans. "It is difficult to stick to the agenda because he makes many digressions. Patient wholly self-absorbed, speaking at length about his accomplishments (teaching, books), ancestry (German royalty), and financial resources ($20,000 from Social Security and his pension, $13 million in book royalties). For him treatment is not an issue. Rather, for him, the main issue is that he is not ill and that his entire history of psychiatric hospitalization is the result of government persecution." Dr. Munson concluded that further hospitalization was needed, given Charles' lack of insight into his illness and his questionable judgment when it came to financial issues, as indicated by his claims to millions of dollars in royalties.

As the weeks passed, the medication began to allow Charles to exercise more control over his behavior. He discussed his delusions with less frequency and he continued to become more social and amiable. Dr. Munson recalled that the improvement in his condition culminated in an unusual role reversal on the ward. A psychiatric aide on the ward at the time was taking college courses in psychology and having considerable trouble with a paper she had written for one course, which she had been asked to rewrite. When she mentioned this to Charles, he offered to help her. They spent several afternoons going over the first draft and her notes. The next week she resubmitted the revised paper and received an "A." Dr. Munson remembered that Charles was pleased to be able to help and to have the opportunity to offer a practical demonstration of his claims regarding his past, and of his potential for the future.

Charles was clearly no longer a danger to himself or

to others. By late October preparations were begun in earnest for his conditional discharge, with a discharge date set for November 28. Despite indications that his condition had stabilized, Dr. Munson was not very optimistic about Charles' prospects following his release. "I thought he would comply with medications under pressure; that eventually the system would get tired of monitoring him and things would slide; and that he would probably get readmitted. The feeling was less a comment on him than on the illness and the system."

A discussion between Charles and a social worker about where he would stay in the community after his release suggested that Dr. Munson was justified in his pessimism. According to his progress notes, Charles told the social worker that he did not need assistance finding a place to live because "his wife has rented herself and Mr. Lachenmeyer a room at the Radisson Hotel for a brief stay after his discharge. He reports that his wife has secured a home in the Grand Isle area of Vermont for herself and Mr. Lachenmeyer to reside in after his discharge, and that their son is going to stay with them over Christmas. Our records indicate that he is divorced and is not in touch with his ex-wife or son. He maintains that this is not true." The social worker went ahead and made arrangements to place Charles in Allen House, subsidized community housing for transients and the mentally ill located near Burlington. Charles then told the social worker that the arrangements were unnecessary in any event because he owned the Radisson Hotel—exactly what he had told Amy King the week before being thrown out of Subway for stealing potato chips.

My father's delusional system had apparently reverted, with the help of medication, to its pre-Commander-in-Chief state, circa October 1993. He believed, as he had one year before, that the abuses he had suffered at the hands of his persecutors were about to come to an end and that what was his by right—a house to replace the house in Pelham that had been stolen from him, compensation for his losses, even the return of my mother and me—would be bestowed upon him immediately following his release from Vermont State Hospital. When I learned that my father had envisioned a family reunion that Christmas, I was struck by the irony that at the time I almost converted part of his delusional beliefs into reality. If I had mailed the children's book I wrote that winter to my father's correct address, he might have received it in time for Christmas and felt at least partially vindicated in his renewed optimism.

Despite the hopefulness of his delusional beliefs, Charles was still afraid of what the future would bring. His progress notes recorded that starting in late October he began to experience debilitating panic attacks, which he described as "jitteriness" and "free-floating anxiety." On ten separate occasions during his last month at Vermont State Hospital he requested and received Ativan, an anti-anxiety medication which can become addictive, to help control his panic attacks. He also reported increased motor restlessness, a side effect

of the Haloperidol, and was given Cogentin to minimize the symptoms. Old coping patterns also began to
reemerge; on a supervised shopping trip with other
patients to a mall, Charles disappeared and, ignoring
hospital regulations, returned with a cup of beer in his
hand.

Charles spent his last weeks on the ward preparing
for his release. He began collating and editing the
hundreds of pages of writing he had done over the
previous ten months. One morning he even visited the
hospital barber shop and got his beard shaved off and
his hair cut for the first time in two years. On his way
back to the ward, he stopped at the clothes rack,
where donated clothes were available for patients who
wanted a change of clothing, and assembled a new
wardrobe. When he walked into the day hall in a
threadbare suit and sat in his usual chair, staff and
patients alike did not recognize him. He was flattered
by their reception. When Dr. Munson told him he
looked like a new man, he smiled and replied, "I
feel like a new man. Now, I have to shave every day."

On November 27, the panic attacks were so bad that
Charles spent most of the day in bed. The next
morning he was released from Vermont State Hospital
in the company of his new case manager. Slung over
his back in a garbage bag was all of his writing.
Although Charles was once again subject to the con-
straints of a conditional discharge and had again been
labeled a paranoid schizophrenic, he had won a battle

on another front. His New Hampshire guardianship had been dissolved, bringing to an end all of his ties to the state of New Hampshire. Charles returned to Burlington, if not a new man, a different man. No one on Church Street recognized him as the tall, unkempt transient who had haunted the Marketplace the previous winter.

Chapter 11

The Untimely

Somehow Charles found the strength to resurrect himself again after his release from Vermont State Hospital on November 28, 1994. He must have looked back that day on the previous nine years' struggle to regain control of his life, following his first release from New Hampshire Hospital, and wondered what he had to show for all of his suffering and the loss of all that time. When he finally gained full access to his funds from New Hampshire the following week he discovered a partial answer: he had accumulated close to eleven thousand dollars in back SSI benefits and pension checks while living on the street. He opened a bank account at the Vermont Credit Union, with which he had not had dealings the previous winter, and rented a small second-floor apartment on Church Street, one block down from his former hangout, Leunigs Restaurant. From his window he could see the street on which he had lived for ten months, the street that had almost killed him.

On his own again, insulated by a roof and four walls, Charles began methodically to rebuild his life. He withdrew three hundred dollars from his bank account and bought an entire wardrobe at Woolworth's, including an inexpensive suit to wear on future job interviews. He spent several afternoons sitting in front of a computer at the local Kinko's, typing from memory a new copy of his résumé, as well as dozens of job query letters addressed to universities throughout New England and New York State. As soon as his telephone was turned on, he called the alumni offices of the Poly Preparatory Country Day School in Brooklyn and the College of William and Mary and requested alumni directories, so that he would be able to approach former classmates about job possibilities.

My father's perspective after his conditional discharge continued to be an uneasy mixture of practicality and delusions. Despite his realistic efforts to rebuild his life, he persisted in his belief that he would be reunited with my mother and me at Christmas. Shortly after moving into his new apartment he called his brother-cousin, Clifford, whom he had not spoken to since the summer of 1992. He did not mention his ten months on the street or his time at Vermont State Hospital. He focused instead on the future, telling Clifford that he was getting remarried to my mother on Christmas Day. Clifford suspected that this was not true, but still thought that my father sounded more like himself than he had in years. They discussed the possibility of meeting sometime in the new year, but did not make plans.

There was only one visitor to my father's apartment in December 1994—his new case manager. Sporting a walrus mustache and a baseball cap, he met me on my last day in Burlington outside the building where my father died. After shaking my hand and expressing his condolences, he presented me with a small oblong cardboard box. Inside were my father's eyeglasses, which had somehow found their way to him after my father's death. The first thought that entered my head was that I was glad that my father had had his glasses while he was living on the street. I could not imagine what it would have been like to live in that hostile, alien world and not be able to see one's enemies clearly. Then a feeling of nausea came over me when it hit me that the glasses I was holding in my hand had rested on the bridge of my father's nose, in life and in death.

Charles' case manager visited him several times after his release from Vermont State Hospital. He had been familiar with his reputation the year before as an unusual and problematic transient on the Marketplace and was impressed by the radical change in his appearance and demeanor. "He went from this very dramatic-looking individual to a very well-dressed, clean-cut individual who could go into any shop and sit and fit in very well. It was like he was a whole different person." Although Charles' case manager smelled alcohol on his breath during those few weeks, he knew nothing about his prior drinking history, and so did not suspect that his transformation might have been less complete than it appeared.

Charles' case manager saw him for the last time on New Year's Day 1995. He recalled that Charles seemed more agitated than usual. "When I got there that morning he had a spiral notebook out which he was writing in furiously. I asked him what he was working on. He said he was writing a book, but he would not tell me what it was about." That same day, Charles sent a letter to the psychiatric aide whom he had helped get an "A," expressing his disappointment that his wife and son had not showed up at Christmas. He also mentioned that his panic attacks had returned in full force, obliging him to spend hours at a time lying in bed.

Charles died the next evening of a heart attack, alone in his apartment. His death was not instantaneous. Police photographs taken at the scene indicate that he had had enough time to register shock before he died. He knew that his life was over before it ended. He knew in that moment that his persecutors had won: after years of incessant struggle there would be no redemption, no eleventh-hour recognition of the accomplishment that his struggle represented, no one to care that it was all coming to an end. He had fought his way back from the furthest reaches—from madness, from homelessness, from frostbite and starvation—only to die, abandoned and forgotten, in a dingy studio apartment in Burlington, Vermont.

If not for an unexpected phone call from a stranger, I would never have learned that my father had been homeless. When the police officer who was handling my father's case called Clifford in January 1995 to inform him of his death, he told him what he had learned about the last two years of my father's life. Out of a sense of compassion, when Clifford told my mother the news, he said only that my father had died of a heart attack, alone in his apartment in Burlington, Vermont—which is what my mother then told me. Two days later I received a call from my father's landlord on Church Street. He wanted to inform me that there was a clause in my father's lease obligating his estate to honor the terms of the lease. Those terms included reimbursement for any damages to the apartment resulting from his tenancy.

The landlord said that there was extensive damage to the apartment, not as a result of my father's tenancy, but as a result of his death itself. He claimed that my father's body had lain undiscovered for several days, and went into graphic detail describing the extent of its decomposition. He said, for example, that the odor resulting from "leakage" was so bad that even after a thorough cleaning and a new paint job he had been unable to rent the apartment. I listened to the voice on the other end of the line and had trouble believing my ears. A complete stranger who lived three hundred miles away was describing in extraordinary detail the condition of my father's body in death—as part of a sales pitch. He wanted me to pay for the cleanup and the intervening month's rent, and to continue to pay the rent until he was able to find a new tenant or until the lease expired, whichever came first. The landlord ended his sales pitch with the threat that he would sue me if I refused, and added for good measure, "I knew your father very well and I know that he would have wanted you to pay me."

I tried to keep my wits about me. I asked the landlord to forward a copy of the lease so I could review it and to also send along my father's effects, C.O.D., including any and all papers in the apartment. He promised that he would send me everything the next day. Instead, he threw out all my father's belongings and mailed me an invoice for the alleged damages to the apartment. In an effort to research the validity of the landlord's claims, I called the police officer who had investigated my father's death. To my relief, he told me that the extent of the decomposition of "the untimely" had been minimal. (An "untimely," he explained, was the police term for someone who has died outside of a doctor's care.) When I refused to pay the landlord, he put a lien against my father's estate, and was eventually awarded the clean-up costs, the security deposit, and a termination fee by the court.

Knowing that I would never see my father's effects, I

asked the officer, before hanging up, to describe in as much detail as he could what had been in the apartment. He told me about my father's résumé, the rejection letters from the colleges, and his spiral notebook. Then he mentioned how puzzled he had been by the contrast between my father's effects and his living conditions. He repeated what he had said when the medical examiner arrived on the scene. "An intelligent man gets down to this point. How did he get to be in *this* apartment in *Burlington, Vermont*?" It was only as an afterthought that he added how surprised he had been when he realized that my father had been a transient on Church Street the year before. Those few words had almost the same effect on me as hearing that my father had died.

I saw my father only one more time after my fourteenth birthday. During the summer of 1990, I decided to take a spontaneous road trip. After briefly consulting a map early one morning, I pointed my car in the direction of Quebec. Six hours later I was driving through the city of Manchester, New Hampshire, in a downpour, looking for a place to grab a quick lunch. While debating the relative virtues of heros and pizza, I remembered that my father had been living in Manchester when I broke off contact a year and a half earlier. His address came to mind, unsolicited: 81 Stark Street, apartment 4B. At that moment I saw the street sign for Stark Street go by.

The coincidence inspired in me a momentary, uncharacteristic belief in fate.

I drove down Stark Street slowly and stopped in front of #81, a small six-story brick building with white trim. I looked out through the rain at the side of the building, found the fourth floor windows, and knew immediately that I was looking into my father's apartment: two windows at the back of the building had been converted into makeshift bookshelves and were completely blocked by row after row of books. I could not bring myself to get out of the car and ring the doorbell, and I could not bring myself to leave, so I backed up and found a parking space which gave me an unrestricted view of the entrance to #81. My heart was racing. I caught myself laughing out loud at the irony that the last words I had written to my father were, "I cannot live in your world; you cannot live in mine." I had been wrong; we lived in the same world whether I chose to believe it or not. The proof was the situation in which I found myself: on my way to visit the country to which my father had once tried to escape, I had accidentally arrived at his front door.

After a while the rain stopped. Only half aware of what I was doing, I started playing one of the solitary games I had played as a kid on long road trips with my parents when I was supposed to be napping: watching rain drops slide down the windshield, I made bets with myself about which drop would reach the windshield wiper first. The key to winning was picking the drop that had the most other drops in its downward path because each time two drops touched they combined and gained momentum. When all the big drops were gone, I moved on to another game. I started lining up the little static beads of water that gravity left behind with the streetlight at the end of the block and watched them slowly turn from red to green to yellow and back again.

Then I saw him. He was twenty yards away, walking in the direction of #81—and my car. From a distance he looked exactly the way he had on my fourteenth birthday. There was nothing about his appearance or the way he held himself that suggested that he was "crazy." I watched him get closer and closer. In the time it took him to cover ten yards he aged twenty years. His hair thinned and wrinkles fanned out across his face. I suddenly realized that he was looking right at me. I tried to make my body conform to the outline of the car seat and did not breathe again until he entered the front entrance to 81 Stark Street, and disappeared from view. He had not seen me after all. I looked up at his windows, hoping that if I saw him again, I would some-how know what to do, but all I could see were his books. It started to rain again. I turned on the windshield wipers, glanced at the building one last time, and drove away.

When I learned, after my father's death, that he had been homeless in Burlington for ten months in 1993, I wondered what my reaction would have been had our paths crossed in 1993 instead of 1990. I had to believe that if I had seen my father sitting on a park bench on Church Street wearing the uniform of the transient instead of walking toward his apartment on Stark Street on a rainy day, I would not have driven off. I would have tried to help him. If the difference between my father in 1993 and 1990 was one of degree, the question arises, at what point on that continuum would I have overcome my fear and self-absorption and approached him? According to his case manager's progress notes from 1990, my father was at that time trying to find the determining point where his thoughts went from being rational to irrational. Ever since his death I have been trying to find the determining point where my thoughts go from being solipsistic to empathetic.

It is inevitable, perhaps, that since my father's death I have also been trying to find that determining point in the people who knew my father, in the people whom I know and count among my friends, in my family, and in strangers. It is an important question to ask, and a frightening one to attempt to answer. Our society's attitude toward and treatment of people with schizophrenia suggests that our ability to sympathize with our fellow man is not determined by his degree of suffering. People with schizophrenia possess the heroism of the terminally ill or the severely disabled who, simply in their determination to survive, are proclaiming their love of life. If anything, their heroism is greater; they are losing to their disorder something even more important than their bodies—their minds.

People with schizophrenia not only face their symptoms; they face pervasive prejudice. Leaving aside the media's portrayal of schizophrenia and the public's ignorance, irrespective of their education or background, of the meaning of the word itself, one need only look at our use of language to see the extent of our prejudice against the disorder and against mental illness in general. Our vernacular speech is rife with expressions that appropriate, belittle, and mock the experiences of the mentally ill: "What are you, some kind of psycho?," "You must be insane," "I'm feeling schizy," and on and on. The mentally ill are the only clearly defined demographic in this country that has not benefited at all from the current overextension of "political correctness." That these kinds of statements are in fact prejudicial can be readily ascertained with a simple test: the next time you hear someone using an expression that appropriates elements of mental illness, try replacing those elements with "cancer" or "AIDS." The humor—the intuitive sense of appropriateness—is gone in a flash because we have been taught that you do not mock someone else's suffering—unless, apparently, it is the result of a mental illness.

The extent of prejudice against people with schizophrenia becomes even more apparent when one removes suffering from the equation. Viewed entirely in economic terms, the amount of funding devoted to research into the causes of and treatments for schizophrenia is minuscule relative to other disorders. Recent estimates from the National Institute of Health indicate that for every dollar schizophrenia costs the US economy, less than one cent is invested in research. In contrast to this, for every dollar cancer costs the US economy, ten cents is invested in research, and for every dollar AIDS costs the US economy, fifteen cents is invested. When I think too long about this or about the overwhelming evidence that sympathy is a selective and, from the perspective of relative suffering, an arbitrary phenomenon, I try to impose on myself a myopic view of reality: I try to remember Jason Palmer's cigarettes, Amy King and John Markey's coffee, the transient who sat next to my father because it was clear that he needed to talk with someone. When that fails, I fall back on the most important lesson my father ever taught me.

The last person I met in Burlington was the police officer who told me that my father had been homeless. I remembered from our conversation two years earlier that he had looked through my father's spiral notebook when he found the body. I contacted him because I wanted to know whether he remembered anything about the contents of the notebook. He did. This is what he told me. "It was endless. Pages and pages. Lots and lots of very big words. I remember journal type entries.

Specific actions that happened that day. A lot of mentions about the Marketplace. For some reason, I remember references to a specific bench. People walking by. There were a lot of references to that bench and to a 'transient' sitting on the bench—he used that word. There was also a lot of stuff which did not make much sense about some kind of scientific experiment that had to do with the bench. I wondered what that was all about."

The officer was the only person who read what my father was working on when he died. Although any chance of knowing for certain what my father thought about his life as the transient was lost with the loss of his notebook, the reference to the experiment indicates that he still believed that he was a victim of Thought Control when he was released from Vermont State Hospital. This, taken together with the references to the transient and the park bench, suggest that his last book was the same book of protest that he had been writing in his head all those months while living on the street, spooled out now with the benefit of paper, pen, and a desk.

I marvel at my father's strength: that he returned to Burlington with his dignity intact, that he had the inner reserves left to once again send out query letters to universities, and that he still had enough faith in himself and in humanity to make another attempt at writing his book. Nothing my father experienced—his transformation into the transient, his subsequent return to the role of patient, the disappointment he felt after his discharge, realizing once again that the experiment was not over—*nothing* had killed his desire to make sense of his world or to again try to communicate his ideas to an audience that had long since forgotten him. He refused to believe that his future was and always would be his past, replayed over and over and over again.

When I look at my own life and the stupid, petty things that knock me off course from time to time, I remember the words that my father wrote to me in a letter in December 1986, when I was seventeen and he was forty-three. "No matter how adverse the circumstances—and mine have been adverse—there is never any reason to give up." There are more reasons to give up than there are to endure—there always have been—and that is one of the miracles of life: that most of us stay the course in the face of disappointment, tragedy, evil, and every event good and bad taking place in the shadow of death. We create strange, complicated fictions—God, love, justice, beauty—which we offer up as enduring truths. We lie to ourselves and we lie to our children. My father lied to me when he wrote that there is never any reason to give up—he tried desperately not to let his dying world taint mine—and that is what made him a good father. He lied to himself by telling himself that he had a reason to believe in his future and in humanity—and that is what made him a good man.

It was my father's example that gave me the strength to survive his death, to survive the discovery that he had lived as a transient in a cold, small city in Vermont, and to write this book. His last, unfinished book and this book are mirror images of each other, reflecting inverted versions of the same experience. It is my hope that in some small way this book complements and completes the book that he was not able to finish. If I could have one wish, it would be that my father were still alive and that there would have never been any reason for me to write this book. Having written it, I want to believe that he would have understood my intentions; that he would have understood that I am not just another co-conspirator trying my best to destroy his world. Even if he would have disagreed with me about which image is reflected and which is real, I want to believe that he would have understood that I love and admire and miss him, and that I have finally learned the lesson he tried to teach me so long ago.

There is never any reason to give up.

Much of the information in the Author's Note is taken from *The Diagnostic and Statistical Manual of Mental Disorders, Fourth Edition,* American Psychiatric Association, 1994. The information on Mary Baker Eddy's life in Chapter 2, "The Outsider," is taken from *The Healing Revelations of Mary Baker Eddy* by Martin Gardner (Prometheus Books, 1993), which I recommend to anyone interested in reading more on the origins of Christian Science.